Reallocating Resources
How to Boost Student Achievement Without Asking for More

Allan Odden
Sarah Archibald

CORWIN PRESS, INC.
A Sage Publications Company
Thousand Oaks, California

For information:

Corwin Press, Inc.
A Sage Publications Company
2455 Teller Road
Thousand Oaks, California 91320
E-mail: order@corwinpress.com

Sage Publications Ltd.
6 Bonhill Street
London EC2A 4PU
United Kingdom

Sage Publications India Pvt. Ltd.
M-32 Market
Greater Kailash I
New Delhi 110 048 India

Printed in the United States of America

Library of Congress Cataloging-in-Publication Data

Odden, Allan.
    Reallocating resources: How to boost student achievement without asking for more / by Allan Odden and Sarah Archibald.
        p.   cm.
    Includes bibliographical references and index.
    ISBN 978-0-7619-7652-3 (cloth: alk. paper)
    ISBN 978-0-7619-7653-0 (pbk.: paper)
        1. Education—United States—Finance—Case studies.   2. School-based management—United States—Case studies.   3. Educational change—United States—Case studies.   I. Archibald, Sarah.   II. Title.
    LB2825 .O312   2000
    371.2'06—dc21   00-008769

This book is printed on acid-free paper.

09 10 13 12 11 10 9 8 7 6 5

Corwin Editorial Assistant:	Kylee Liegl
Production Editor:	Nevair Kabakian
Editorial Assistant:	Candice Crosetti
Typesetter/Designer:	Lynn Miyata

Reallocating Resources

CONTENTS

ACKNOWLEDGMENTS

The issue of resource reallocation in education is new and controversial. We would not have been able to write this book unless teachers and administrators in schools around the country were engaged in this process. Thus, we first would like to thank the teachers and principals in the schools studied, as well as their superintendents and central office staff, for spending time with us describing what they did and why they did it. It should be clear from what we say in the book that these individuals are pioneers in the education system on this topic. We have the utmost respect and admiration for these folks at the cutting edge, and we encourage them in their efforts. We hope that our descriptions of what they are doing are accurate and convey the exciting substance of what they are trying to accomplish—teaching students to the level of higher performance standards using mostly the funds that they currently have.

We would also like to thank John Anderson and the staff at the New American Schools (NAS); leaders of the school designs that NAS sponsored; and teachers, principals, and central office leaders in the districts that have partnered with NAS, all of whom provided Allan Odden with the initial opportunities to examine how schools could use resources differently. As written elsewhere, the way these new school designs use resources is quite different from traditional schools, and schools adopting these designs and engaging in the program restructuring and resource allocation necessary to put the designs into place represent another set of schools and education leaders at the forefront of education reform.

We also are indebted to Dr. Anita Tychsen, a former PhD student in the Department of Educational Administration at the University of Wisconsin–Madison, who initially studied a number of the schools profiled in the book. Her work has contributed immensely to the substance of this manuscript. In addition, we want to acknowledge the research of Dr. Karen Hawley Miles, an independent consultant who is one of the few other individuals around the country who has been conducting research on resource reallocation in schools. She also has been working with principals and teachers in several urban districts to design strategies to use resources—both time and money—more productively. We have benefited immensely from all of the work she has done and the conversations we have had with her.

We would like to thank Lisa Armstrong, the administrative assistant in the University of Wisconsin office of the Consortium for Policy Research in Education. As usual, Lisa was responsible for putting the manuscript into final form, spent time tracking citations we could not find, and used her winning personality to encourage us to complete the book when we didn't think we had either the time or the energy to do so.

Finally, we want to acknowledge our primary funding source for this effort, the Office of Educational Research and Improvement in the U.S. Department of Education. This work was supported by the Consortium for Policy Research in Education (CPRE); Grant No. OERI-R3086A60003 from the National Institute on Educational Governance, Finance, Policy-Making and Management; U.S. Department of Education, Office of Educational Research and Improvement; and the Wisconsin Center for Education Research, School of Education, University of Wisconsin–Madison.

—Allan Odden
Sarah Archibald
Madison, Wisconsin
January 2000

Corwin Press would like to acknowledge the following reviewers:

Rustin Clark
Moundridge Unified School District 423
Moundridge, KS

Carolyn Herrington
Florida State University
Tallahassee, FL

David W. Messer
Maryville High School
Maryville, TN

Lawrence O. Picus
University of Southern California
Los Angeles, CA

Paul G. Preuss
Herkimer BOCES
Herkimer, NY

Ross Rubenstein
Georgia State University
Atlanta, GA

Joseph Waler
Trinity High School
Garfield Heights, OH

Donald L. Walters
Temple University
Philadelphia, PA

ABOUT THE AUTHORS

Allan **Odden** is Professor of Educational Administration at the University of Wisconsin–Madison. He is also Co-Director of the Consortium for Policy Research in Education (CPRE), which is funded by the U.S. Department of Education; the director of the CPRE Education Finance Research Program; and principal investigator for the CPRE Teacher Compensation project, funded by the Pew Charitable Trusts and the Carnegie Corporation. CPRE is a consortium of the University of Wisconsin–Madison, the University of Pennsylvania, Harvard University, the University of Michigan, and Stanford University. Formerly, he was Professor of Education Policy and Administration at the University of Southern California (USC) and Director of Policy Analysis for California Education (PACE), an educational policy studies consortium of USC, Stanford University, and the University of California, Berkeley.

He is an international expert on education finance, school-based financing, resource allocation and use, educational policy, school-based management, teacher compensation, district and school decentralization, education incentives, and educational policy implementation. He worked with the Education Commission of the States for a decade, serving as assistant executive director, director of policy analysis and research, and director of its educational finance center. He was president of the American Educational Finance Association in 1979-1980 and served as research director for special state educational finance projects in Connecticut (1974-1975), Missouri (1975-1977), South Dakota (1975-1977), New York (1979-1981), Texas (1988), New Jersey (1991) and Missouri (1992-1993). He was appointed Special Court Master to the Remand Judge in the New Jersey *Abbott v. Burke* school finance court case for 1997 and 1998. In 1999, he was directing research projects on school finance redesign, resource reallocation, and teacher compensation.

x

Dr. Odden has written widely, publishing more than 170 journal articles, book chapters, and research reports, as well as 20 books and monographs. He has consulted for governors; state legislators; chief state school officers; national and local unions; The National Alliance for Business; the Business Roundtable; New American Schools; the U.S. Congress; the U.S. Secretary of Education; many local school districts; the state departments of education in Victoria and Queensland, Australia; and the Department for Education and Employment in England.

His books include *School Finance: A Policy Perspective* (2nd ed., McGraw-Hill, 2000), co-authored with Lawrence Picus; *Financing Schools for High Performance: Strategies for Improving the Use of Educational Resources* (Jossey-Bass, 1998), with Carolyn Busch; *Paying Teachers for What They Know and Do: New and Smarter Compensation Strategies to Improve Schools* (Corwin Press, 1997) with Carolyn Kelley; *Educational Leadership for America's Schools* (McGraw-Hill, 1995); *Rethinking School Finance: An Agenda for the 1990s* (Jossey-Bass, 1992); *School Finance: A Policy Perspective* (McGraw-Hill, 1992), co-authored with Lawrence Picus; *Education Policy Implementation* (State University of New York Press, 1991); and *School Finance and School Improvement: Linkages for the 1980s* (Ballinger, 1983).

Dr. Odden was a mathematics teacher and curriculum developer in New York City's East Harlem for five years. He received his PhD and MA degrees from Columbia University, a Masters of Divinity from the Union Theological Seminary, and his BS from Brown University.

Sarah Archibald received her MA degree in policy analysis from the La Follette Institute of Public Affairs at the University of Wisconsin–Madison. She also received her BA from the University of Wisconsin–Madison. Ms. Archibald is currently a full-time researcher at the Consortium for Policy Research in Education at the University of Wisconsin–Madison. Her research centers around school finance policy issues such as resource reallocation, school restructuring, and adequacy. Her writing on these topics has been published in a number of different publications. She is also involved in some aspects of CPRE's teacher compensation studies. Anxiously awaiting the birth of her first child, she expects to complement her research and policy interests with all the joys of parenthood in just two short months.

INTRODUCTION

Why Reallocate Resources?

Why should schools reallocate resources? That is a very good question. Many in education would argue that the issue is not reallocating current resources but getting more resources. In the long run, we probably agree with that claim. But in the short to medium term, we have concluded that current resources can and must be used better if current education reform goals are to be attained. Furthermore, our research is showing that districts and schools—administrators, principals, and teachers—play the key roles in determining how to use current education resources better.

For the past decade and a half, the American public schools have been engaged in a major reform effort. Although many would say that American public schools are always engaged in reform (Tyack & Cuban, 1996), the fervor of reform during the 17 years since the 1983 *Nation at Risk* report has been intense.

Today's reform goal is to teach all students to high standards. There is more than one message embedded within this phrase. One message is that reform is focused on all students, or at least all but the most severely disabled students. A second is that high standards are required—high standards for the curriculum content that is taught and high standards for the student performance that is measured. A third is that the education system can accomplish this goal. And a fourth message, particularly relevant to the topic of resource reallocation, is that the goal can be accomplished with current resources, including the modest increases in resources that public schools generally receive annually.

Putting some numbers on these phrases helps to show how ambitious the reform goal is. The National Assessment of Educational Progress (NAEP) is the country's best indicator of the level of student achievement. Recent NAEP trend analyses (Campbell, Voelkl, & Donahue, 1998) suggest that across all subjects and across all grade levels, about 25% of students achieve at a level that NAEP terms "proficient." Although there is some controversy over how NAEP defines proficiency, we accept the current NAEP definition. "Teaching all students to high levels" literally means that the education reform goal is to increase the proportion of students achieving at or above proficiency to 50%, 75%, and even 90%. Just increasing the percentage to 50 would mean doubling education results; increasing the percentage to 75 would entail tripling education results. These are ambitious goals.

One should not focus too much on this quantifying of the education reform goal. The general notion is that student performance—student achievement in academic subject areas—should rise substantially. The hope, moreover, is that the performance of all categories of students—those in cities, those in rural areas, those from low-income backgrounds, those with mild learning disabilities, those who are learning English, those in the bottom half of current achievement levels—will rise by significant amounts. Thus, there is also an equity element embedded within the reform goal.

But the reform goal is rarely accompanied by a "fiscal note," which is legislative lingo for identifying the cost of achieving such a goal. We believe that the assumption of education policymakers across the country is that education reform is to be accomplished primarily with the dollars and resources already in the education system. So, the reform goal really is to teach all students to high standards with current levels of resources.

This adds an additional set of meanings to the current education reform goal. Doubling or tripling performance results means that the current education system must become much more effective and efficient; performance must be raised dramatically while all education tasks are improved. Put differently, the productivity of the education system must be improved drastically. The only way that education performance can rise by a factor of two to three within the current budget is to increase the productivity of current dollars.

To be sure, this analysis makes the education reform goal even more ambitious—some might say impossible. But even given this productivity improvement imperative, few educators want to back off from the reform goal. The choice for educators is to either improve education system productivity or decide that they do not want to teach all students to high standards. Given this choice, most say, "Let's go for it. Let's try and at least make progress toward the goal. Let's improve the productivity of our schools." Whether this perspective will raise the performance of all students to high levels is a question we will be able to answer only in the future. But this shift in thinking does help make movement toward that ultimate goal possible.

This book, informed by empirical research, is about how schools have begun to improve student achievement results with their current levels of resources through a program restructuring and resource reallocation process. We have many exciting stories to tell. We have many successes to describe. The schools that we and others are studying show that the education dollar can be spent more wisely, in new ways that actually boost student academic achievement. Although the schools studied have not taught all students to high standards, they are teaching more students to higher standards, and they are doing so with the same level of resources. This book uses the information collected from the various schools that have been studied, but rather than telling their stories in the form of case studies, we have written a sort of how-to guide for principals, teachers, and others interested in engaging in school reform.

Reasons to Engage in Resource Reallocation

Schools decide to engage in restructuring and resource reallocation for a variety of reasons. Here, we list five common rationales for change, many of which may be similar to those in your school or district.

First, many schools are buying into the current standards-based education reform agenda. In doing so, they support the curriculum content and student performance standards adopted by their districts and states. They also share the goal of educating their students to the new, higher standards. And, as schools assess their previous programs, curricula, and education strategies, many find them wanting. Common problems include a lack of the rigor and cohesion necessary to produce the higher level of results desired. As a result, schools begin to search for a better curriculum, more cohesive strategies, and more integrated ways to organize and structure their educational programs. Adopting new standards seems to be a good place to start, because it tends to raise the bar for what teachers teach and what students learn.

Second, many schools are dissatisfied, sometimes deeply so, with their strategies for serving special needs students—students from low-income backgrounds, students for whom English is not their native language, and students with mild learning disabilities. Moreover, many schools have concluded that because the past strategies did not work for their previous goals, they definitely would not be sufficient to reach their new goals. For this reason, teachers and principals around the country are resolving to find better ways to serve students with special needs.

Third, many schools are hearing multiple messages from the district, state, and even federal government that school-level reform is required. The federal government is encouraging school sites to use Title I for schoolwide programs, not for the traditional pullout services providing remedial mathematics and reading instruction. States are also supporting more school-based education reform efforts. Many states have begun to administer a new federal program offering Comprehensive School Reform grants. This program provides planning and training grants to schools that adopt or create whole or comprehensive school reforms that integrate all programs and strategies around a single education vision. These policy initiatives reinforce the findings from school improvement and school change research that school improvement occurs one site at a time, albeit within local and state education systems. This research also shows how there can be different school strategies that are all focused on producing student performance within a common set of standards (Ross, Sanders, & Stringfield, 1998).

Fourth, district offices around the country are altering practices to provide schools with more authority and responsibility. Some districts are deciding that because schools may be better able to maximize budget efficiencies than the central office, they should receive lump-sum budgets and discretion to reallocate their budgets for different strategies. Still other districts are beginning to implement school-based management in a more general sense, where the district or state sets core goals and measures results, but schools determine how to accomplish those goals. In some cases, districts are making more drastic changes, such as reconstituting failing schools and implementing new strategies that they believe will help those schools succeed. Whatever the specific circumstances, it is clear that many districts are focusing attention on individual school sites and requiring each site to determine how it could improve its own performance.

Finally, performance levels in the majority of our nation's schools are not as high as the schools themselves would like them to be. Whether performance is low overall and needs to be much higher to meet the standards, or the performance of certain categories of students is low and the faculties believe it could be higher, the result is the same. A number of changes must be made at the school level to promote higher student achievement.

In sum, districts and schools around the country are in a position where they want to improve student performance substantially. These educators share a common context, one in which high standards are beginning to be set, restructuring agendas are being encouraged, schools are being given much more budgetary and decision-making authority, and there is an understanding that dramatic school improvement (within a standards and accountability framework) is an individual school process. And for the most part, schools are expected to make improvements with the resources they already have.

The Book in Brief

This book reports both on the beginning results of a long-term study by the Consortium for Policy Research in Education (CPRE) on resource reallocation to support higher student achievement, and on studies of resource reallocation conducted by others (e.g., Miles & Darling-Hammond, 1998). All of the schools studied engaged in resource reallocation as part of an overall school agenda. In a sense, resource reallocation is the finance side of school-level restructuring. The CPRE foray into this fascinating topic was identifying the cost structure of various whole school designs offered by the New American Schools (Stringfield, Ross, & Smith, 1996). In several studies, Odden (1997a, 1997b) and Odden and Busch (1998) showed that the cost structure of these schoolwide strategies was different from the traditional school in America and that all designs could be financed by the average elementary, middle, or high school in the country through a resource reallocation process. Odden, Archibald, and Tychsen (1999) showed that even the lowest spending districts in one Midwestern state could afford the most expensive of these designs, again through a resource reallocation process.

Although there has been receptivity to the notion of school-level resource reallocation, there has been a dearth of information on how resource reallocation can actually be accomplished. In a previous CPRE study, Miles and Darling-Hammond (1998) described how a number of schools, including both elementary and high schools, reallocated resources in urban districts across the country and also improved student learning.

The purpose of this book is to draw from all of the research on resource reallocation around the country to show how resource reallocation looks "on the ground." Our goal is to describe actual resource reallocation practices and the realities of the resource reallocation process using examples from the schools that we have studied, as well as schools that others have studied. Although it is helpful to know that resource reallocation is feasible, it is even more helpful to principals and teachers to know about the nitty-gritty details of resource reallocation—which resources get reduced, which resources are added, what funding sources are tapped, what problems are encountered, and how the process unfolds in real school settings.

This book begins to provide this knowledge. Drawing from studies of schools and districts actively engaged in both school restructuring and resource reallocation, this book lays out the steps that would be necessary for other schools to follow a similar path. Although most of our examples derive from the schools studied during the past several school years, we incorporate strategies for resource reallocation identified in other research as well.

All types of schools have been studied, including schools in urban, rural, and suburban districts; large and small schools; and schools in large, medium, and small districts. The schools represent a range of student demographics, with high, average, and low percentages of both minority students and students eligible for free and reduced-price lunches. Some of the schools had more than 25% of their students with some type of disability, with others having less than 10% of such students. In most of the schools, initial student achievement was low. So, we and others have studied schools that needed to improve performance dramatically, and schools that faced difficult circumstances in doing so.

Each school adopted a number of new educational strategies, each of which required various expensive educational ingredients—smaller classes, more planning time, expanded professional development, tutoring for students who were struggling to achieve to high standards, and so on. This book tells the story of how schools can finance expensive program needs by describing the vast array of decisions that must be made, including how to pay for the new strategies.

The potential for using resources differently to improve student achievement is not only an important initiative being undertaken at the school and district level, but it is also now a part of the required school finance reforms in the state of New Jersey. In 1998, the New Jersey Supreme Court ruled that the state had provided sufficient funds to the 28 urban districts that were the focus of that state's school finance controversies. It decided that the funds already provided were sufficient for those schools to adopt a whole school reform, such as the Roots and Wings program, and implement that program through restructuring and resource reallocation. In effect, the court ruled that although schools would need to use their dollars differently, they had sufficient funds to finance that program, which is one of the most expensive school strategies in the country (Odden, 1997a). Although implementation has been difficult (Analt, Goertz, & Turnbull, 1999), the fact remains that resource reallocation is a central element of one state's school finance court mandate for the first time in this century. Thus, knowing the substance of how resource reallocation can proceed and to what end is important.

The remainder of the book has six chapters that outline the overall process and identify numerous program restructuring and resource reallocation practices. These chapters show that these two elements go together: Schools reallocate resources for the needs of their new educational strategies. Without a new educational strategy—or vision—schools would not have had a road map for which resources to drop and which resources to add.

Chapter 1 focuses on the change process itself and describes why and how schools engage in program restructuring and resource reallocation. As we learned, restructuring programs and reallocating resources constitute a complex, large-scale change process. Each school studied underwent a fairly complex change process, and Chapter 1 describes this important process.

In order to guide the resource reallocation particulars, schools need a new vision, what we call a new educational strategy. This requires decisions about the regular education program, as well as about programs and services for special needs students—those eligible for state or federal compensatory education dollars, those for whom English is not their native language, and those with learning disabilities. Chapter 2 discusses decisions that must be made about the regular education program and how the various schools studied adopted, adapted, or created curriculum and instructional strategies.

Chapter 3 takes these core educational strategy decisions and shows how they determine the cost structure of a school, and thus how a school would need to use its resources to finance various strategies. The chapter covers such issues as how students will be grouped, overall class sizes, planning and preparation time, and professional development. Traditionally, these resource decisions are not made consciously; this book illustrates how doing so can follow a school's decision on its overall education agenda and largely determine its funding needs.

Chapter 4 describes the resource requirements of the various choices that schools make about serving special needs students. The fact is that all schools have some percentage of struggling students—students who need extra help to learn to district or state performance standards. The amount of additional assistance necessary varies widely, from one-to-one tutoring to a self-contained classroom. Thus, all schools need some strategy—or set of strategies—to help these students. As this book shows, a number of expensive new strategies that serve this purpose can be funded via resource reallocation. These changes often are accompanied by a series of new policies as well, ranging from requirements for teacher licensure to enhanced teacher training. This chapter describes many of these innovative educational efforts.

Chapter 5 discusses the resource reallocation strategies that can be employed to pay for all of these new educational programs. It also addresses the sources of funding that are most commonly tapped for reallocation. But more importantly, it discusses resource reallocation by the categories of staff in most schools—regular classroom teachers; regular education specialists (art, music, physical education); categorical program remedial specialists (compensatory education, bilingual education, special education); pupil support specialists (guidance counselor, nurse); instructional aides; and other staff (clerical, custodial). Thus, this chapter shows how schools can reallocate the staffing resources within their schools to help fund school reform. And, because the majority of a school's budget is spent on staff, the ability to reallocate some staffing resources helps explain the extent to which schools are able to employ a resource reallocation strategy. This chapter is written for principals, teachers, and district administrators who are not budget experts, but who know the kinds and levels of staff in their school and can link staffing with program needs.

Finally, as a way of summarizing the resource reallocation processes that have taken place at the sites discussed throughout the book, Chapter 6 takes a closer look at two sites and examines exactly what was reallocated to implement their new educational strategy. Moreover, we discuss how those changes have affected student achievement at those sites, and we give examples of other sites that have boosted student achievement through resource reallocation and restructuring. Chapter 6 also describes the various district contexts in which schools operate. From these examples, we identify several new roles for districts in supporting school-level program restructuring and resource reallocation.

Although we are bullish on the possibilities that these schools show for how schools can use current resources better, we end this chapter with a point made at the beginning. The schools studied have improved performance, sometimes dramatically, using mostly their current resources. We expect that they can continue to improve performance in the next year or two. But we do not know if they can teach all of their children to their state and district proficiency standards with their current level of resources. If they can, terrific. But if they cannot, then at least they can say they improved performance with the dollars they had, and then make a strong case for why they need more dollars, and how they would spend them.

CHAPTER ONE

Step 1:
The Change Process

There are many reasons that a school might engage in reallocating its resources. Often, some sort of catalyst pushes the school to this point, whether it is consistently low reading scores in elementary schools, poor high school student performance that cannot be defended despite complicating circumstances, or a new district strategy of school-based budgeting. In the schools studied, it was often these forces working together that precipitated the decision to engage in the deep and fundamental change that is necessary in program restructuring and resource reallocation. Although the stimulus for change can begin at the school or district level, schools that receive the support of their district undoubtedly have a better chance at sustaining meaningful change over the medium to long term than schools that do not.

In the previous chapter, we outlined several reasons why the schools that have been studied engaged in resource reallocation: dissatisfaction with current levels of student performance; even greater dissatisfaction with traditional approaches to serving special needs students; getting the full message of standards-based education reform and realizing that current instructional strategies for both regular and special needs students were not sufficiently powerful to meet the goals; and understanding several messages from federal, state, and district governments that school-level restructuring was desired.

In a sense, then, the schools were pressured from multiple sources to engage in both rethinking their overall educational strategies and making the related fiscal changes required to fully implement those strategies. In short, the schools were ready to engage in a large-scale, fundamental change process. In this chapter, we discuss what the literature has to say about large-scale organizational change, and we describe the practices we observed at various sites for creating and sustaining meaningful educational change.

The chapter has three sections, which represent the three stages of the large-scale educational change process:

▶ Lay the foundation for change

▶ Create a new educational strategy

▶ Implement, monitor, and improve continuously

Lay the Foundation for Change

As is true in other arenas, educational change is often spurred by recurring problems. Low academic achievement, lack of leadership at the school site, and teacher dissatisfaction are just a few of the problems that may prompt districts and schools to make major changes. But such changes need to be managed in order to make the overall restructuring and resource reallocation process successful. Researchers who have studied large-scale organizational change identify three key steps in this process (Mohrman & Cummings, 1989). Although they did not explicitly refer to the research on large-scale organizational change, nearly all of the schools studied nevertheless followed this three-step change process fairly closely.

The first step is called laying the foundation, which consists of

> determining the values toward which the organization will be re-designed, acquiring learning and awareness about organizational design principles and alternatives, and diagnosing the current organization to gain awareness of the gap between the way the orga-

nization currently functions and how it needs to function to successfully achieve its values, given its environmental and technical requirements. (Mohrman, 1994, p. 206)

For schools and faculties undergoing such a change process, this step includes analyzing demographic and achievement data about the student population, reflecting on the values of the staff and school community regarding education and its purposes, and reaching a consensus as to the school's priorities for the future. This step can be referred to by a number of different names, including needs assessment and self-study.

Undergoing a needs assessment helps a school identify its strengths and weaknesses, thereby highlighting the areas that need to be the focus of change. But most importantly, analyzing data on all aspects of the school helps the school understand the specifics of student performance by different content areas and different topics within each academic subject; how performance differs by race, income, and gender; the specifics of student attendance and mobility; and what parents think about the school.

Such a data analysis exercise also produces two other elements that support school change. The first is school ownership of the data and the conclusions that are made. The fact that the school faculty identifies and describes the strengths and weaknesses of the school itself helps to remove the tendency to deny the need for change or the existence of problems. Second, the process creates the thorough and detailed understanding of the school that allows the faculty to better match new educational strategies with the actual needs of the school.

For many schools, this data analysis process can take up to a full year, and shortchanging this analytic step could prove detrimental to the success of the reforms that are chosen. The new strategies that schools choose must meet their particular needs in order for faculties to be strongly committed to them and to conclude that the change is worth the effort. To ensure that this happens, a deep and sound understanding of a school's needs and a solid match with a new educational strategy are critical.

Nearly all of the schools studied conducted some sort of needs assessment. But one of the most comprehensive processes took place in a district we will call Cordell Place, which made a year of self-study a prerequisite for gaining control of school funds and engaging in program restructuring and resource reallocation. Because this district's needs assessment was so thorough, we describe it in detail here as a model for other districts and schools to follow.

Cordell Place's new superintendent and other district leaders decided that their schools' low levels of student performance were unacceptable and needed to be raised. Because many of its schools qualified for significant amounts of federal Title I monies, and could use those funds for schoolwide programs because their student poverty concentration exceeded 50%, the district decided to launch a major change process by offering these schools complete control over their Title I dollars. But the district set a condition. In order to gain discretion over Title I funds, schools had to agree to explore the possibilities for resource reallocation in an analytical manner by means of a self-study.

The self-study included an investigation by these schools' faculties of their student population, including attendance, mobility rates, and, most importantly, student achievement. Various data were collected; both teachers and parents were surveyed. All of the information was analyzed by each school's faculty for the purpose of identifying the characteristics of the student population and then setting realistic achievement goals. After the schools could describe the characteristics of their students with confidence, the district advised the schools to identify research-based strategies that would address their school's needs. If they could do so, they were then free to use Title I money to support that design or strategy.

Many of the school staff members who participated in the self-study attested to the value of the process, saying that it forced them to take a closer look at their students—demographic information as well as information regarding student mobility, attendance, and achievement—and learn who they were and what their academic strengths and weaknesses were. School staff members were able to dismiss anecdotes that other stakeholders used as suggestions for change in favor of data-driven conclusions derived from their own analysis of quantitative and qualitative student information. In the process, they discovered that they could make more informed decisions about what areas of the curriculum should be given special attention, as well as what social and community needs had to be addressed. Given this detailed picture of their schools, staff members felt well equipped to investigate curricular programs that had proven effective elsewhere and that fit their needs and their school philosophy.

Schools in other districts engaged in similar data analysis processes. One elementary school's faculty began analyzing student performance data, the perceived and actual effectiveness of their strategies for helping students with special needs, and the satisfaction of both teachers and parents. They then organized two retreats to discuss this analysis with parents.

They identified several different elements that were problematic with the school and assigned them to different parent/teacher committees. The proposal for improvement from all committees was to reduce class size, a strategy that the school implemented the following year.

Another school became embroiled in a reconstitution process. After being identified as having consistently low levels of performance, the school was slated for reconstitution. A four-person district team consisting of two representatives of the teacher union and two administrative representatives orchestrated the reconstitution process. After assessing the characteristics of the student population, this team selected a new educational strategy for the school. In particular, it selected the Expeditionary Learning/Outward Bound design (http://www.elob.org) and augmented it with both a strong reading program (First Steps) and a strong mathematics program (TERC). The team then selected a principal who was committed to the design. The principal, with the approval of the team, selected lead teachers who also were committed to the new educational strategy. Finally, the principal and lead teachers selected the remaining teaching staff, who all came aboard knowing exactly to which educational strategy they were committing and why. In this case, even though the school staff did not get to select the new strategy, the hiring process ensured that all staff were invested in the new strategy.

Thus, the first step in laying the foundation for change is critical in establishing a shared outlook for the direction of organizational change. As Mohrman cautions, "Skipping this stage results in different participants enacting their different understandings and being at cross purposes . . . [and] failure to establish such an integrated understanding early in the change process leads to conflict and disillusionment" (Mohrman, 1994, p. 206).

Create a New Educational Strategy

The second step in the change process requires analysis of the organizational elements that can produce performance improvements in the desired areas. At this stage, participants in the change process choose the elements of the school that need changing in order to fix what needs to be fixed in the organization. Mohrman warns that laying the foundation (the first and previously described step) must be done in a comprehensive manner in order for this stage to be successful, or else

> various change efforts in the organization will be designing changes that do not complement one another. The organization will have to recycle into a stage of clarifying values and identifying criteria. The design piece of large-scale change is much easier if there are agreement and understanding of the criteria for successful change. (Mohrman, 1994, p. 208)

In other words, participants in the change process must spend time reaching a consensus for a unified vision of the future of the organization, as described in the previous section. Then, having assessed the needs of the school and researched strategies for improvement, the next step is to choose the full complement of educational strategies that best meet the needs of the school.

Creating a new educational strategy requires consciously making decisions about the regular education program, as well as about programs and services for special needs students. There are many decisions that must be made about the regular education program. The first task is to decide on the overall curriculum and instructional strategies. Some schools selected one of several existing national, comprehensive school designs (see http://www.nwrel.org/scpd/natspec/catalog/index.html for a list of such designs). Others adapted pieces from different designs. Still others adopted a more rigorous curriculum, program by program. And a few schools were successful in creating their own standards-based curriculum units.

Each school's educational strategy also required conscious attention to several related issues that largely drive a school's cost. For example, a school that identifies low reading scores as the most glaring need will want to consider the most effective reading program, the ideal reading class sizes, the best ways to group students for reading, and the professional development that teachers will need to teach the new reading program successfully. Many of the schools studied identified low reading scores as the number one problem that needed to be addressed, but they took a variety of approaches to restructuring their reading programs. Some adopted a research-proven program, such as Success for All (e.g., http://www.successforall.net). Other schools implemented small class sizes of 15 and also adopted a new, more phonics-based reading curriculum. Both decisions had cost implications. The former required tutors and schoolwide instructional facilitators, and the latter required more teachers; both required extensive professional development. Schools made these decisions consciously and were aware that they would need to reallocate resources to implement them.

The schools also made dramatic new choices about serving special needs students. Of course, all had some percentage of struggling students, or students who needed extra help to learn to the level of the performance standards. Moreover, the new strategies that most schools implemented did not make fine-lined distinctions between a low-achieving student, a struggling student from a low-income background, a student who had to learn English as well as academic content, and a student with some type of mild learning disability. The schools viewed all of these students as struggling to meet the new and higher performance standards, and therefore, they used their new educational strategies to help all of these students. Furthermore, as described later in this book, some schools pooled the funds that accompanied these different student labels in order to afford the more powerful strategies of their new educational program.

Although the amount and specific type of additional help needed by each student varied widely, most schools dramatically reduced or eliminated the pull-out resource room strategies with which they were dissatisfied. (Those students with severe disabilities continued to be served in self-contained classrooms and thus were not affected by the school restructuring or resource reallocation process.) The schools then implemented some combination of one-to-one tutoring, instruction in small classes of about 15, or some other new strategy. And each particular strategy for struggling students had the goal of educating those students to the same high performance standards as all other students.

Several schools moved pull-out teachers, who had dual licensure in both regular and special education, into regular classrooms and mainstreamed all but the severely disabled students. This practice also enabled schools to reduce class size by increasing the number of classroom teachers. And by adopting a dual licensure strategy for its teachers, the schools ensured that the expertise needed for each class of students was in place.

Schools also made decisions about how to use teachers' time. Several schools rescheduled the teaching day to provide 90 minutes of planning time at least four times each week. Other schools altered the schedule so that all teachers on the same teaching team had their preparation period at the same time to enable them to meet as a team. Some schools added time to 4 days and then dismissed students early on the fifth day, thus giving teachers 2 to 3 hours of uninterrupted planning time. Nearly all schools created and implemented new strategies for giving teachers more uninterrupted and often collaborative planning time during the regular school day to provide the time for preparation and professional development needed to implement their new educational strategy.

Many other strategies that serve this purpose can be funded via resource reallocation; the important thing is for schools to identify the ones that meet the needs of their students and then staff and structure the school accordingly. These changes often are accompanied by a series of new policies as well, ranging from requirements for teacher licensure to enhanced training.

By structuring, scheduling, and staffing the school according to the imperatives of their new educational strategy, the schools began allocating resources to where they were needed most and could have the largest impact on achievement. Without a new educational strategy, or vision, schools would not have known which resources to drop and which resources to add.

Implement, Monitor, and Improve Continuously

The third step in a large-scale organizational change process, which certainly describes both school restructuring and resource reallocation, is implementation, monitoring, and continuous improvement. Schools start implementing their new educational strategies, they attempt to monitor both the extent of their implementation and the early effects on student performance, and they seek to maintain and improve their strategies.

It should be clear that this third step is not the same as simply implementing a new educational strategy. To be sure, the schools studied all began implementing their new educational strategy. And they exerted efforts to ensure that they were fully implementing all elements of their new educational strategy, in part because they knew from reviewing research that full implementation was required in order to produce the desired effects (Cooper, Slavin, & Madden, 1997; Haynes, Emmons, & Woodruff, 1998; Huberman & Miles, 1984; Stringfield & Datnow, 1998).

But even though all of the schools had put together a new educational strategy that they believed would help them improve their students' performance, the level of performance improvement that they needed to produce was often greater than their selected strategy had produced in other schools. Thus, the schools believed that their new educational strategy would begin to improve student performance, but they also knew that they would need to do even more—that full implementation of their new strategy was necessary but not sufficient to achieve the goals that they were trying to attain.

For example, several schools studied began the restructuring and resource reallocation process by implementing the Success for All reading program. This required a complete change in their reading program, new forms of student grouping including cross-grade ability grouping for reading, more professional development, a full-time instructional facilitator, and tutors. Initial implementation required substantial program restructuring and different use of school dollars.

But in the second year, some schools decided to strengthen the program by, for example, adding an additional teacher tutor. Other schools that had been using the reading program for 1 to 2 years decided to adopt the Roots and Wings mathematics program as well. Many of these same schools were planning to add the integrated science–social studies World Lab program in the fourth and fifth years. In short, although the schools began with a fairly bold restructuring plan for reading, they extended and improved it over time by changing other core curricular areas as well.

The schools that had adopted a class size reduction program also began analyzing their reading and mathematics curriculum programs more seriously. Although they had bet almost their entire school budget on the small class size strategy, they soon realized that small classes alone might not be a powerful enough change. Some concluded that small class sizes together with a stronger reading program, in which all teachers would be trained, would likely be even more effective than just small classes per se.

We also heard hints from some teachers that spending the bulk of the school budget on small class sizes might not have been the best strategy. They wondered whether classes in the range of 20 students (i.e., smaller than 25 to 30, but larger than 15), together with some teacher tutors for struggling students, might be a stronger strategy than very small classes for all subjects every day, without any additional support for struggling students.

Because the schools studied tended to be in their second or third year of implementation, we cannot say for sure what might happen in subsequent years. But we can raise the above cautions and make the following suggestions. Each school needs to monitor the results of its efforts on student performance each and every year. The schools need to know whether the new strategies that they are implementing are having the desired effects, and in which areas they are not, and they also need to be aware of other issues and challenges as they arise.

School restructuring to produce the goals of current standards-based education reform is not a 1-year, or even a discrete 2- or 3-year, effort. It might take an entire generation. Therefore, schools need to view themselves as engaging in an ongoing restructuring, analysis, monitoring, and improvement process, that is, a continuous change process.

To be sure, it is imperative that schools start with a good understanding of their current situation and a strong belief that the new educational strategies they select will improve their students' learning dramatically. But not all programs will be as effective as desired. Furthermore, conditions and demands can change, and midcourse corrections may be required. Thus, the third part of the change process is recognizing that the kind of improvement in performance required by current standards-based reform will require schools to engage in a continuous change process over numerous years.

Summary

It should be clear that engaging in program restructuring and resource reallocation constitutes a large-scale change effort. Schools contemplating tackling this agenda would be smart to understand this fact and to design and manage a careful change process. Significant time should be spent laying the foundation for the change by engaging all key actors in analyzing school-specific data. This gives school faculties a comprehensive and detailed understanding of conditions at the school, particularly the nature and level of student performance. Next, faculties should spend time trying to match a new educational strategy with the conclusions from the data analysis. Finally, schools should understand that the full implementation of the new strategy is required in the short term, but, that over time, it might need to be augmented and changed in order to produce the higher levels of performance required.

All three steps of this complex change process are critical. Throughout this book, you will note references to the steps that schools must take to help ensure the success of their chosen reforms. In the next chapter, we describe in more detail the decisions that must be made when choosing a new educational strategy.

CHAPTER TWO

Step 2:

Defining a New Educational Strategy

The hallmark of a successful school is a powerful educational strategy. Developing or choosing a school's educational strategy—its overall curriculum and instructional program, its approach to helping struggling students achieve to standards, and its professional development system—is one of the most important tasks for a school seeking to raise its level of performance. Furthermore, the educational strategy will direct both program restructuring and, as we shall see, resource reallocation.

Although this book emphasizes the resource reallocation required to make many different kinds of changes, it is the educational strategy that is the key to improved student performance. Indeed, Newmann (1996) and Newmann, Lopez, and Bryk (1998) found that schools that were most successful in improving student achievement were those that implemented authentic instruction. Elmore and Burney (1996) found that an intense, consistent, and relentless focus on improving instruction was successful in Community District 2 in New York City; the district produced among the highest scores when they administered the New Standards assessments in 1998.

Conversely, it has been the lack of focus on the educational strategy that has been the bane of many school reform efforts. Elmore and Peterson (1996) found that the schools least successful under school-based management were those that did not focus on instruction. Murphy and Beck (1995) reached the same conclusion after reviewing scores of school-based management efforts and, in a subsequent book (Beck & Murphy, 1996), showed how having an educational agenda was one of the key factors that made school-based management work.

Our previous chapter also showed that a search for a new educational strategy was one of the first steps in beginning the resource reallocation process. Crafting this new educational vision was key, and the more thoroughly and thoughtfully schools engaged in this process, the stronger their attempts at school reform became.

Selecting the Core Curriculum and Instructional Program

One important part of making changes to promote higher student achievement is to adopt or design a cohesive curricular strategy, one that is linked to state and district standards and equips teachers to help students succeed. This means creating or selecting curriculum strategies in at least the core disciplines of mathematics, science, social studies, and language arts.

On one hand, this task seems trivial. All schools have some sort of curriculum program. But under the assumption that it is instruction, or what is taught, that is the school factor most linked to what students learn, selecting a curriculum and instructional strategy is critically important.

Indeed, one of the prime lessons from the Third International Mathematics and Science Study (TIMSS) is that what is taught accounts for the major differences in student achievement across countries (Schmidt, McKnight, & Raizen, 1997). Disparities in student achievement, which are quite large, are not strongly related to length of school day or year, or hours spent watching television, which are the most popular culprits, but, rather, the content of the curriculum. Thus, deciding what a school's curriculum strategy should be becomes a crucial decision.

Schools involved in resource reallocation, like other schools, have essentially used a number of different methods for implementing a new curriculum strategy. One is to develop their curriculum program locally, on their own, and the second is to adopt externally developed curriculum programs. Furthermore, schools that reallocate resources to reduce class size seem to select the former, whereas those that adopt an externally developed school design tend to choose the latter. However, there are exceptions. One class size reduction school we studied adopted externally developed reading and mathematics programs, whereas several comprehensive school designs, such as the Coalition of Essential Schools and the Co-NECT design, which are supposed to have a standards-based curriculum as their core element, actually require substantial curriculum development by school staff.

Many of the schools studied adopted a whole school design that includes a comprehensive school curriculum. For example, several schools initially adopted the Success for All reading program and, after a couple of years, decided to adopt the more encompassing Roots and Wings design. Success for All is a complete elementary school reading curriculum, with a variation for schools with children whose native language is not English; research has shown that schools implementing this reading program have significantly improved student achievement in reading (Slavin & Fashola, 1998), including schools with many English language learners (Slavin & Madden, 1999). Roots and Wings includes not only the Success for All reading program, but also the Math Wings mathematics curriculum program and the World Lab program, which is an integrated science–social studies curriculum strategy. Schools implementing all three curriculum programs have also improved student performance (Slavin & Fashola, 1998; http://www.naschools.org; http://www.successforall.net).

Other elementary, middle, and high schools that we know are engaged in resource reallocation have adopted other comprehensive school designs that are accompanied by a fairly complete curriculum strategy, such as the Modern Red Schoolhouse and Audrey Cohen College (Stringfield et al., 1996). Modern Red, which is partly based on Core Knowledge standards (Hirsch, 1996), includes curriculum units in the core disciplines of mathematics, science, social studies, and language arts, as well as art and music. Modern Red also includes many performance assessments that schools can use to determine the degree to which students have learned the concepts in any curriculum unit. So, at least three comprehensive school designs— Roots and Wings, Modern Red, and Audrey Cohen College—include specific curricula in the core content areas.

The creators of the elementary Roots and Wings design have also developed a comprehensive strategy for both middle and high schools called Talent Development Middle and Talent Development High Schools (http://www.csos.jhu.edu/Talent/middle.htm and http://www.csos.jhu.edu/Talent/high.htm). Again, these whole school designs include curriculum approaches in mathematics, science, social studies, and language arts. There are several other comprehensive school designs that include a specified core curriculum program with their design, including High Schools That Work (http://www.sreb.org/Programs/hstw/high.html), America's Choice (http://www.ncee.org/ac/intro.html), and the Edison Schools (http://www.edisonschools.com).

By contrast, other schools have gone the "grow your own" curriculum route. For example, two of the class size reduction schools that we studied adopted this approach. One of those schools, which had about 25% of its students with limited English proficiency, grouped its students by ability for reading classes. These reading classes were designed to align with the district content standards. The school complemented this reading strategy with similar efforts in mathematics, science, and social studies. A second class size reduction K-8 school modified its core curriculum, aligning it with state and district standards and making it compatible with its inclusion approach for its learning-disabled students.

A third strategy is for a school to adopt curriculum programs content area by content area. Many sources provide information for schools wishing to go this route. The Northwest Regional Education Laboratory has developed an Internet-based catalog of both curriculum programs and school designs (http://www.nwrel.org). The U.S. Department of Education is about to release a series of reports, discipline by discipline, on curriculum programs that it has concluded are effective (Viadero, 1999). A panel recently reviewed the quality of several mathematics curriculum programs (U.S Department of Education's Mathematics and Science Expert Panel, 1999). One class size reduction elementary school we studied adopted one of these proven curricula. It not only reallocated its resources to reduce class size to between 15 and 18 students, but it also selected two core curriculum programs to ensure better success in reading and mathematics— the First Steps reading program (http://www.nwrel.org/scpd/natspec/catalog/firststeps.htm) and the TERC mathematics program (http://www.tercworks.terc.edu). Both are described in the Northwest Labs catalog, and both have been successful in various school settings.

We know that many other schools are selecting both school designs and specific curriculum programs. For example, the San Antonio school district adopted a policy of having each school select and implement a comprehensive school design *and* decided that having a specific reading and mathematics curriculum could strengthen many designs. So, the district adopted the Macmillan reading program and the Chicago Mathematics curriculum (http://www.nwrel.org/scpd/natspec/catalog/univchicago.htm, which they have since changed to Harcourt-Brace) and required all elementary schools to implement them. It turned out that sites that had already adopted school designs such as Co-NECT and Expeditionary Learning (Stringfield et al., 1996), which have a project approach to curriculum, ended up with a stronger curriculum strategy with both their school design and a specific curriculum in these two core areas.

High schools can adopt curriculum programs as well. For example, many high schools have adopted the International Baccalaureate curriculum out of the desire to have an instructional strategy that meets international standards for rigor. Other high schools have as a goal that all of their students will take Advanced Placement courses offered by the College Board. Both of these are options for the High School Academy of the Edison Schools.

What binds together all of the above strategies is a school's decision to have a common, schoolwide approach to curriculum and instruction that will be used by all faculty. These decisions constitute the core of their educational strategy. Faculties in such schools collectively believe that if they implement these new instructional approaches, student performance will rise.

As a caution, we should state that it is difficult for schools to create their own curriculum program. Developing an entire schoolwide curriculum takes time, effort, and expertise, which do not exist in sufficient quantities in all schools. Only schools with specially trained faculty should even consider developing their own curriculum or school designs that require considerable curriculum development, such as the Coalition of Essential Schools (Sizer, 1996). For most schools, this might be an overly ambitious and risky strategy.

Having made this point, none of the school designs and none of the externally developed curriculum programs is meant to be teacher proof. All of the above instructional strategies require thoughtful application in their day-to-day implementation, with teachers having to make dozens of specific decisions as they lead classes of students through various curriculum units. Furthermore, all teachers and faculties can tailor and adapt any externally adopted curriculum program. Indeed, the Co-NECT and Expeditionary Learning designs provide teachers with wide latitude in developing the appropriate projects within which to implement even an externally developed curriculum, such as Chicago Mathematics.

Finally, every school's curriculum, whether adopted, adapted, or created, needs to be aligned with its state's and district's content and performance standards. Indeed, producing this alignment was a task in which every school we studied engaged. Because this task is so important in a standards-based education environment, it is another reason why even adopting externally developed curriculum programs—whether part of a school design or whether adopted on a content-by-content basis—requires teacher effort in curriculum adaptation and a change in their day-to-day teaching practices.

A Strategy for Struggling Students

In addition to a core curricular strategy, schools need to identify specific strategies for providing students who struggle to perform to high standards with the extra help they need to do so. All of the schools we studied wanted struggling students—whether they were low achievers, needed to learn English, or had a specific learning disability—to meet the performance standards expected of all students. The schools also were universally displeased with their previous programs for struggling students, which tended to rely heavily on two strategies: (a) remedial instruction provided by a licensed specialist in a pull-out resource room, or (b) remedial help provided by an instructional aide inside the classroom. Neither approach had been successful in having students who are struggling meet performance standards.

We found two quite different approaches to a revised strategy for struggling students. Several schools adopted a tutoring strategy in which trained and licensed teachers provided students who were falling behind with individual, one-to-one tutoring to help them catch up. In most cases, this tutoring was provided early in a student's career, in grades 1, 2, and 3.

The second strategy was simply small class sizes. All of the class size reduction schools we studied believed that with smaller classes, the regular teacher could provide both the regular instruction for all students and the extra help that struggling students needed.

Both of these strategies—licensed teacher tutors and small class sizes—are expensive. In most settings, these strategies are deemed possible only with extra money. But all of the schools we studied implemented these expensive strategies with very little extra money. Through resource reallocation, these schools adopted expensive and what they believed were new and powerful strategies to ensure that struggling students also performed to expected levels.

We should note that not all comprehensive school designs have an explicit strategy for struggling students. Furthermore, some of these designs have agreed that they need to be augmented by such a program. The Modern Red Schoolhouse design sanctions a reading tutoring program for students struggling to read. The Comer School Development Program has added a tutoring laboratory for reading that includes a lead tutor, instructional aides as tutors, and volunteer tutors. In addition, as New Jersey has implemented its court-ordered school finance reform, which requires each school to adopt and implement a comprehensive school design, it has included five teacher tutor positions for each elementary school (with 500 students), regardless of the specific school design selected (Analt et al., 1999). The tutor positions are a resource within the budget to be deployed by each school however it decides to structure an explicit strategy for struggling students.

A caution must also be raised about the class size reduction strategy being a sufficient strategy for struggling students. To be sure, there is research that documents the efficacy of small classes, particularly for low-income and minority students in grades 1-3 (Achilles, 1999; Grissmer, 1999). However, we do not have explicit research that this strategy *alone* is powerful enough to have all students learn to standards. As we mentioned in Chapter 1, some of the teachers in schools with small classes wondered whether class sizes of 20 with some tutoring strategy would be a smarter approach. At this time, we cannot answer that question, but we thought it necessary to raise as an issue.

Finally, although there is research that trained and licensed teachers are effective in tutoring students in reading (Wasik & Slavin, 1993), we have some evidence that the typical instructional aide may not be as effective as a licensed teacher tutor (Shanahan, 1998). As far as we can determine, the only teacher-aide-as-tutor program that has shown substantial positive impact on student achievement is the one developed by George Farkas (1998, 1999). This program has a rigorous literacy screen for selecting such tutors, the tutors are given multiple weeks of training in a specific reading-tutoring program, and they are closely supervised. Several schools we studied had instructional aides provide reading tutoring. Although the aides received some training, the training was not extensive, they did not employ the rigorous selection process used by Farkas, nor was there the same de-gree of supervision. We would expect such an approach to tutoring to have less of an impact on student achievement. All of these issues are discussed in greater detail in Chapter 4.

Teacher Professional Development

The third critically important component of a new educational strategy adopted by the schools we studied was a new approach to providing teach-ers with a sufficient amount of professional learning opportunities, that is, the strategy to ensure that teachers have the knowledge and skills they need to teach the new curriculum successfully. In a 1999 poll of more than 1,000 K-12 teachers, 80% reported needing more time to learn new practices with their colleagues, reflecting the necessity of providing professional development when implementing a new educational strategy (Bradley, Hoff, & Manzo, 1999).

All of the schools we studied that were engaged in substantive resource reallocation also reallocated resources to support intensive (and costly) professional development strategies. For all schools studied, the nature and type of professional development was coupled with their core educational strategy on two levels.

On one level, faculty in the schools simply believed that they needed to improve their overall instructional expertise. They knew that one of the core shortcomings with their school in the past was its instructional pro-gram, and they believed that improving instruction via intensive profes-sional development had to be a priority.

On another level, all schools deployed professional development activi-ties that were focused on particular characteristics of their curriculum and instructional approaches. For example, two of the class size reduction schools found it necessary to adopt a policy whereby all of their teachers would be dually certified in the future. First, they wanted all teachers to have the regular classroom teaching license so that even if they had formerly worked in resource rooms, they were qualified to teach a whole classroom of students. Second, they wanted all teachers to have the additional expertise required for their overall educational strategy to work. The school that incorporated students with minor learning disabilities into the regular classroom adopted a policy that all teachers should be certified in regular and special education. The school that eliminated English as a Second Language (ESL) pull-out programs wanted teachers to be licensed in ESL in order to accommodate the special learning needs of those students in the regular classroom. Thus, they invested in the professional development needed to produce this extra expertise.

Three other schools provided professional development that was directly linked to the reading program that was part of the overall school design they had adopted. This training occurred over a 2-year time period. Moreover, two of these schools had decided to implement the mathematics program that was part of their adopted school design and, in the year of our study, had begun the 2-year effort to provide the training for all of their teachers in the mathematics curriculum program.

In addition to these substantial expansions of professional development, nearly all schools also provided additional forms of training for teachers. Several had programs where teachers could identify specific, individually focused professional development needs that were aligned with the new school strategy and engage in the programs that met those needs, with the school covering the costs.

Moreover, most of the schools also provided 1- to 3-week summer professional development institutes that provided both leadership and instructional training. These were in addition to training sessions and follow-up networking activities supported during the school year. The summer programs, which were expensive, were further evidence of the priority these schools placed on intensive training as part of their restructuring and resource reallocation strategies.

Secondary schools that were engaged in restructuring and resource reallocation also invested heavily in professional development. For several high schools, one goal for creating smaller school units was to help create "professional communities" of the faculty within each unit. This is an explicit purpose of the Talent Development Middle and High School organizations, as well as of the organization of the Coalition of Essential

Schools. Professional communities are characterized by teachers working together on curriculum change. Creating schoolwide committees to develop the purpose aspects that cut across each traditional content area is one of Audrey Cohen High School's strategies to engage teachers in professional development (Stringfield et al., 1996). Finally, the Talent Development Middle School provides 30 to 38 hours of professional development per academic subject per year for at least 2 years. This professional development focuses on content knowledge, instructional strategies, classroom management, and modeling of upcoming lessons (http://www.csos.jhu.edu/Talent/middle.htm).

Although structured in various ways, these examples show that all schools provided professional development that was intensive and long-term, included follow-up in teachers' classrooms, and was instructionally embedded in the daily work of teachers, all characteristics of professional development that research shows is effective (Cohen & Hill, 1998; King & Newmann, 1999; Loucks-Horsley, Hewson, Love, & Stiles, 1998). All of these aspects are important because we define effective professional development as any that leads to change in classroom practice that, in turn, produces improvements in student academic achievement.

Summary

Later in the book, we write about how the time and dollar resources were found to support the ambitious initiatives discussed in this chapter. But it should be clear that all schools made heavy monetary and time investments in professional development as a key component of their restructuring and resource reallocation efforts. Professional development was not an afterthought or add-on; it was a core piece of these schools' new programs and was important enough to garner significant funds.

CHAPTER THREE

Step 3:

Organizing and Staffing the School to Support the New Educational Strategy

In this chapter, we discuss how schools organized and staffed themselves to implement new educational strategies. As we describe the various options, we will essentially be identifying the cost structure for a school. And although we will be explicit in these descriptions about which cost elements require additional resources, Chapter 5 tells the fiscal story of how resources were reallocated to support these new strategies. This chapter specifies the cost structure elements themselves. In addition, this chapter identifies several different mechanisms that schools developed to provide the time for teachers to engage in the planning, curriculum development, professional development, and other teamwork required for effective school restructuring.

This chapter discusses the following organizational and staffing issues in turn: determining regular class size and student grouping for instruction, creating the time for professional development and team planning, and identifying the costs of the professional development provided to ease the

31

implementation of the new educational strategy. The final section addresses school size and discusses how several high schools have broken large high school buildings into small units.

Class Size

The primary decision that affects overall school costs, and the context within which instruction will be delivered, is regular class size, or the number of students that are assigned to each classroom teacher. When class sizes are smaller, school costs generally are higher; when class sizes are larger, school costs generally are lower.

Most of the schools we studied—and most schools adopting and implementing a higher performance school design—provided regular class sizes of about 25 students. This should not be confused with a pupil-staff ratio, which is the ratio of all students in a school to all licensed staff in a school, whether or not they teach a full classroom of students. By class size, we mean the actual number of students assigned to a classroom teacher during a given class period. And for most schools, that was about 25. Thus, a school with 500 students and actual class sizes of 25 would need 20 classroom teachers.

But we studied many schools that reduced class size far below the standard of 25 students. Moreover, reducing class size is a very popular policy issue across the country at this time. About half the states have enacted—and funded—class size reduction strategies during the past 5 years (Odden & Picus, 2000). The federal government, largely at the initiative of the Clinton administration, is also interested in class size reduction. In 1998, that administration initiated a strategy to hire 100,000 additional teachers for the nation's schools to reduce class size to about 18 in the early elementary years.

Nearly all of the class size reduction policies have been inaugurated because of a growing belief that lower class sizes improve student learning. Although the research findings that support this belief have been somewhat mixed, today, most analysts—and policymakers—point to the results of the Tennessee class size reduction experiment in the late 1980s as the substantive rationale for this policy. This experiment represents one of the few large-scale, randomized, controlled experiments in education. Thousands of kindergarten through third-grade students in scores of schools all across the state were randomly assigned to small classes (of between 13 and 17 students), regular-sized classes (of between 22 and 26 students), and regular-sized classes with an instructional aide. After 4 years, the results showed that students in the small classes learned more; the effect size was about 0.25 standard deviations—a significant, though modest, effect (Achilles, 1999). The effect was larger for low-income and minority students; some analyses showed that the effect was about twice as large for these students—close to 0.5 standard deviations (Achilles, 1999; Grissmer, 1999). There was virtually no impact on the classrooms with instructional aides.

We studied several schools that were aware of this study and, for reasons particular to each school, decided to implement a small class size policy for students in every grade. For example, one school was a K-2 elementary school, with an enrollment of about 360. It reduced its class size to about 16 students in all grades; doing so required it to hire four additional teachers over its regular allocation of 18 teachers. Another school, serving about 700 students in grades K-8, adopted the same policy for grades K-5. Because its K-5 student population was 326, it needed to hire eight additional teachers over its normal allotment of 11 teachers in order to provide all teachers with a maximum of 17 students.

Miles and Darling-Hammond (1998) studied two schools that adopted a similar class size reduction policy. A special elementary school of 90 students, about one third of whom had disabilities, reduced class sizes from 25 to about 15, which required an additional two teachers. A high school actually reduced class sizes from the normal of 30 in the district to about 18. Achilles (1999) provides several additional examples of schools that reduced class sizes to around 15 students. Finally, we know of an urban district in the Midwest that has decided to reduce the size of all classes to 15 students in grades K-2 in those elementary schools with 40% or more of their students eligible for free and reduced-price lunches (i.e., from low-income families). As in the previous class size reduction examples, this district is able to implement this change without raising tax rates.

In short, all of these schools implemented the typically expensive policy of dramatic class size reduction by reallocating teacher resources that were already in the school (i.e., without additional funds). Chapter 5 describes the details of how they accomplished this extraordinary feat. The purpose here is simply to state that studies have identified a number of schools that have provided quite small classes by using the dollars in their schools differently. It is important to emphasize that these schools provided small classes for all elementary-level teachers for the entire school day: All regular academic subjects were taught to classes of approximately 15 to 18 students.

Still other schools that we studied reduced class sizes only for particular subjects, mainly reading. Two elementary schools provided class sizes of less than 20 for their daily 90-minute periods of reading instruction by having not only the regular classroom teachers, but also several other licensed staff—reading tutors, art and music teachers, and so on—teach reading during the 90-minute reading instructional time block. Thus, these schools were able to provide small classes for reading, which they believed was the most important subject on which to focus their efforts and is the subject for which the research is strongest in terms of the impact of small class size.

One of the elementary schools we studied actually reduced class sizes below the level of 15 for the lowest performing students in grades 1-3. Again, by requiring nearly all licensed staff in the school to teach reading during the 90 minutes of reading instruction, this school actually provided reading class sizes of 10 to 12 for the students having the most difficulty learning how to read. This school also assigned the most skilled teachers to these classes, teachers with either additional expertise in teaching reading or with an additional licensure in learning disabilities. Thus, this school provided highly trained teachers for the most difficult students in the smallest classes—all by reallocating resources. This illustrates the kind of smart use of resources that some would argue represents the best chance the country has of meeting the goal of teaching all students to high standards.

Facilities. Of course, a big question that is always raised about the small class size strategies is, Where did the schools find the space? Generally, this was not a problem! In some cases, classrooms were divided into two, and teachers taught in teams in order to share space effectively and make class size reduction possible. One school was successful in passing a referendum to build a new school in order to make the reduced class sizes possible. But overall, the schools we studied did not have significant problems finding classroom space—and none was underenrolled. The schools simply began using space differently.

As we show in Chapter 5, many of the teachers who were reallocated for regular classroom teachers had been using rooms for other purposes. Because these teacher positions were eliminated, their rooms became available for regular classrooms. For example, if a remedial reading teacher position was eliminated, and that position turned into a classroom teacher position, that teacher's room could be converted to a regular classroom, thus providing space for class size reduction.

We had thought that implementing smaller classes would be more difficult for small schools. As we indicated earlier, one of the class size reduction schools enrolled just about 360 students. But even this school was able to reduce class sizes to 16. Yes, this required some teachers to share classrooms, and the school had to use all spaces—including the library and lunchroom—more efficiently, but it was able to find the space. In fact, the year this school implemented the class size reduction policy, it grew by 40 students, so it had to find two additional classrooms. It found even that extra space and still implemented its small class size policy.

Let us give you another example of why space might not always be a problem. Recall that we know of a district reducing class size to 15 for its schools with 40% or more students qualifying for free or reduced lunch. Initially, the district concluded that there was insufficient space. But on further analysis, they found that a "used" classroom was a space for one teacher. The room was considered used even when the students were gone from the classroom for their "specialist" classes, which occurred at least once—and sometimes twice—during the day. The classroom was unused during lunch. And in this district, teachers had a full afternoon off each week for additional planning time, and the room was considered used during that time as well. In short, a used room was used only about 65% to 75% of the time. The district decided to increase that to closer to 100%. In part, they were able to do so by having the art and music teachers travel to the classroom for the specialist classes, thus freeing up art and music rooms.

The above are just examples of ways in which schools and districts found space. These examples illustrate that each school that decided to reduce class sizes somehow found the space to do so. To be sure, the strategy would be harder, if not impossible, for a growing school with all rooms fully used. This happened in many California districts as they began reducing elementary class sizes in the late 1990s. Often, schools needed to lease portable classrooms. The leasing strategy allowed them to provide small classes quickly, rather than waiting a long time for the capital construction money required to build additional, permanent classrooms.

Grouping practices. Once these basic class size decisions were made, the schools studied also used a variety of different strategies for grouping students for instruction. The grouping practices entailed nearly all of the different types of grouping strategies. Although no grouping strategy varied the costs for any school, which is largely determined by the overall class size decision, it is interesting to note the varied student grouping practices used.

Most schools grouped students into traditional, heterogeneous, same-age classes for most of the day. Many of these schools, however, grouped students by reading achievement level *across grades* for reading instruction, following the literature on the most effective elementary school grouping for this important subject (Slavin, 1987). Some also provided two within-class groups for mathematics instruction (Slavin & Karweit, 1985).

Several schools adopted different versions of multiage student grouping for the entire day, sometimes having students in these groups for 2 years. Many of the high schools that have been studied adopted various forms of block scheduling. However, research shows that, except for the elementary reading and mathematics groupings, the positive claims for these student grouping strategies might be somewhat overstated (O'Neil, 1995; Pisapia & Westfall, 1996; Rettig & Canady, 1999; Slavin, 1990, 1993; Veenman, 1995). The same research, however, also shows that multiage grouping and block scheduling do not have negative effects on achievement, so there is little downside risk to such grouping practices.

In sum, the schools studied implemented a wide variety of student grouping practices, all based on the theory that they would be better than traditional practice. And none of the grouping strategies increased overall school costs; they just represented different and, in some instances, more effective ways to group students for instruction.

Finding Time for Planning
and Professional Development Time

One of the most fascinating aspects of the research on school restructuring and resource reallocation has been the varied and comprehensive approaches that all schools have adopted to provide planning time for teachers and extensive professional development. Although this component of school operations often gets shortchanged in many schools and districts, the schools studied took this issue seriously and invested extensive resources in it.

First, all of the schools employed additional teachers in special subjects in order to release classroom teachers and provide planning, preparation, and professional development time for classroom teachers during the regular school day. This strategy generally required the schools to hire an additional 20% of teachers. So, for example, if a school had 20 classroom teachers, they hired four additional teachers. At this level of additional staffing, each classroom teacher was provided approximately one period (30 to 55 minutes) per day for every day of the week for planning and preparation time.

Generally, these specialist teachers provided instruction in art, music, and physical and library education. When students had these special classes, the regular classroom teacher was released from instructional tasks during that time. Although the subjects taught by the specialist teachers tended to emphasize the traditional special subject areas, there was also variation. For example, one school with discipline problems hired a social skills teacher instead of an art teacher.

One reason that it is not too surprising that schools reallocating other resources did not change their use of specialist teachers is that the school faculties considered the special class subjects—art, music, and so on—to be important in their own right, and they were unwilling to merge them into classroom instruction with the more academic subjects of reading, writing, mathematics, science, and social studies. Another reason is that the planning time provided by those teachers—one period a day for every classroom teacher 5 days a week—was required by the teachers' collective bargaining contract. Although there may be other ways to provide this planning time, the schools we have studied have been reluctant to make any real changes in this area.

Of course, providing some time during the school day for planning and preparation is just Step 1 in providing the time necessary for successful implementation of these new school strategies. Step 2 is to schedule that time in a way that allows teachers to work together, a topic addressed next.

Finding blocks of time. A question that is almost always raised about schools engaging in the kind of program restructuring and resource reallocation that we describe is how teachers found the time to engage in all of

the instructional and noninstructional decision making, planning, preparation, and professional development activities. A partial answer to that
question was just given: Most of the places studied had specialist teachers
on staff who provided regular teachers at least one period per day each day
of the week for such activities. But the schools did more than just provide
this time. They also increased this time and scheduled it more effectively
using a variety of strategies.

First, most schools scheduled all teachers on the same teams for the
same free period. This allowed the teachers to meet and engage in various
activities as a team. Some of the scheduling was incredibly creative for
schools where teachers were part of two or three different decision-making
teams. Grade-level teacher teams might be scheduled for common planning
time 2 days a week. Then, content teams (math, science, etc.) might be
scheduled for a common time on a third day, leaving time for other teams
to be scheduled for common time on the other 2 days. Furthermore, the
most effective schools were very clear that the agendas for each team had to
be attended to, thus not letting student discipline problems or other subjects dominate the action for all team meetings.

Second, schools devised many additional strategies to provide teachers
with more preparation time during the school day. One common strategy
was to have teachers extend the school day for 30 minutes for 4 days and
then release the students for 2 hours in the afternoon of the fifth day, which
provided an extended time period for planning, preparation, and professional development. Although this type of strategy requires parent sanction
and cooperation from the district, especially in situations where students
are bused to and from school, it nevertheless is a strategy widely used across
the country—and it does not require additional resources! This approach provides all teachers with 2 hours of uninterrupted planning time once a week,
and at no additional fiscal cost.

Another strategy was to have teachers voluntarily begin school an hour
before students arrived or remain at school for an hour after students left.
Yes, this represents additional time, but the teachers in such schools simply
said that the job they wanted to accomplish required this extra time. Even
though they might have a period free each day, and sometimes even a free
afternoon, they said that the ambitious restructuring in which they were
involved could not be done within that time constraint.

Some schools devised even more creative ways to carve out the time
that teachers needed. One high school did two things that provided signifi-

cant teacher planning and preparation time. First, students had a block of free time each day to engage in extended self-study. During these study times, they were not supervised by a licensed teacher. Second, students in the same school were required to perform service activities and engage in learning activities off the school campus, that is, in different locations around the community. Again, not all of these ventures were directly supervised by a licensed teacher. Both of these components of the instructional program released teachers from instructional responsibilities and provided time for them to engage in planning, preparation, and professional development. This additional time was especially necessary because this school was implementing a complex integrated curriculum program that required this type of intensive planning. Therefore, by finding a way to provide these extensive time blocks to teachers, the school did what it needed to do to implement its new curricular strategy.

Another elementary school in an urban midwestern city set a goal to provide 90 minutes of uninterrupted planning time for each teacher team 4 days each week. This district is not a high-spending district, so the goal was ambitious. Moreover, the school also increased student instructional time, making the scheduling of the 90-minute planning time even more complex. An explanation of how the school planned to provide this preparation time follows.

First, prior to the new plan, students were scheduled for classes for 6 hours each day, and teachers were scheduled for 7 hours. This structure provided 60 minutes of free time each day for teachers. This time, combined with a planning period during the day and some creative scheduling, could have provided the desired 90-minute planning block. But the school chose not to do this because part of its new educational strategy was to extend the students' instructional time by 1 hour per day. In order to provide the additional hour of instruction, the school changed the student schedule to 8 a.m. to 3 p.m., the same as the teachers, thus eliminating that built-in hour of preparation time.

Next, the school set aside 8 a.m. to 1 p.m. as an *uninterrupted* academic instructional block each day. Instruction in reading, mathematics, science, and social studies was provided during these 5 hours. Teachers and students then had lunch from 1:00 to 1:30 p.m. After that, all classroom teachers had 90 minutes of planning time from 1:30 to 3:00 p.m. The most creative part of the schedule was how the school planned to provide this free time for all classroom teachers each afternoon.

The school took three full-time specialist teacher positions that were part of its regular budget and converted them into 10 part-time positions at 0.3 FTE (full time equivalent) for each part-time position. The plan was to have the 10 part-time teachers provide all of the supervision and instruction during the afternoon time from 1:00 to 3:00 p.m. In addition, because a teacher at 0.3 FTE works for 2 hours and 15 minutes per day, these teachers were also in charge of making sure students got on the buses between 3:00 and 3:15 p.m.

Of course, it does not work for both the teachers and the students to begin their day at 8 a.m., so the school required teachers to arrive at 7:45 a.m. instead. The school then compensated teachers for that extra time by allowing teachers to leave at 1:45 on Friday afternoons, while still allowing them the four 90-minute blocks of planning time each week.

However, the school was unable to implement the plan fully because it could not find the 10 part-time teachers. Nevertheless, the plan shows how it might be possible for a school to provide these large amounts of planning time and also extend the students' instructional time by an hour each day— all without spending additional money.

Another elementary school in a large midwestern city wanted to provide a 90-minute planning block to each grade level 5 days each week. Their strategy was to schedule the normal planning period either right before or right after the teacher's lunchtime. Although this required teachers to eat during their 90-minute planning block, the teachers decided that this was a small price to pay for the benefit of a very long, uninterrupted block of planning time.

However, as was the case with the other school that tried to schedule 90-minute blocks of planning time, this school was not able to implement this schedule for a number of reasons. First, if specialist time for each grade level was provided at the same time each day, the plan would allow only two grade levels to have the common planning time backed up with lunch, one grade with the specialists covering their classes before lunch and another after lunch. Second, if the grade levels were to rotate having specialists backed up with lunch, the school could not meet the goal of providing five 90-minute blocks of planning time for every grade level each week.

Therefore, the school had to compromise its original goal and implement a plan that provided each grade level at least one 90-minute block of planning time per week, with a specialist covering one of the two periods backed up with the teachers' lunch. This strategy, however, required each grade to have special classes at different times each day during the week. Initially, this was viewed as problematic because teachers felt that elementary students liked and needed a consistent daily schedule. But as the plan was implemented, the school discovered that students were easily able to handle the differing daily schedule.

Another school in the same district was able to implement a 90-minute planning period backed up with lunch for each grade level by scheduling lunch at different times for different grade levels. For grades K and 1, lunch was from 11:05 to 11:45 a.m., and the planning period was from 11:50 a.m. to 12:35 p.m. For grades 2 and 3, lunch was from 11:50 a.m. to 12:35 p.m., and the planning period was from 12:40 to 1:20 p.m. For grades 4 and 5, lunch was from 12:40 to 1:20 p.m., and the planning period was from 1:20 to 2:10 p.m. In this way, every grade was able to have a 90-minute planning period when teachers decided to use lunch for this purpose.

We should note that the latter two examples are derived from research conducted by Karen Hawley Miles, and that the district was a strong union district. We should also note that teachers in the school proposed this schedule and use of lunch, which was beyond what was required by their union contract. The teachers placed a high priority on long, uninterrupted planning periods and were able to find the time by using free time and specialist-provided time creatively.

In short, schools devised numerous strategies to provide significant time periods for planning, preparation, and professional development (see Office of Educational Research and Improvement, 1996). In all of the instances we have studied so far, faculties were helped in this creative process by having specialist staff already included in the regular school budget; these positions provided at least one period (30 to 55 minutes) of planning time each day during the week. And through creative scheduling, teachers were often able to find even more time for these important tasks. When asked whether it was worthwhile to give up their lunch period, nearly all of the teachers said some version of, "Yes, this does represent my having to use time for planning that was previously a free period, but the time expenditure is worth it because it has helped us make great strides with student performance."

The Edison School. Those who are familiar with the Edison School design know two things. First, the cost structure and use of time is quite similar for their primary, middle, and high school academies. Second, for all three models, the school day is extended to 8 hours and the school year to 11 months for all teachers. To compensate for this extra time, Edison increases the average teacher's salary to about 16%-18% above what the school district in which the school is located has been paying. It should be clear that this schedule, requiring both more hours during the day and more days during the year, almost by definition provides more time for planning and preparation because students are not involved in instructional activities more than they are in a typical school. Indeed, Edison would say that it provides each teacher 1 hour each day for professional development or planning.

Although we have not been able to study the precise details of the Edison fiscal strategy for funding the extra teacher salaries, which compensate for the extra teacher time, we know it is some variation of the strategies we describe in Chapter 5 for the schools we have studied. In any case, the Edison School provides teachers at least 1 hour of planning and professional development time each day each week, again through a reallocation of resources.

External and internal training investments. Not only did the schools provide the time required for the extensive planning, curriculum development, and training that teachers needed, but they also invested large amounts of additional resources for the kinds of extensive professional development and training that research suggests works. That is, professional development that leads to a change in classroom practice that subsequently results in higher levels of student achievement. For example, several of the schools that had adopted the Success for All reading and Math Wings programs spent $50,000 to $70,000 annually for ongoing professional development and materials from the creator of that school design. Needless to say, these amounts represented a substantial increase from what the schools had been spending for those purposes prior to engaging in resource reallocation and restructuring.

One elementary school of about 300 students spent approximately this amount of money on professional development and training. They provided a 3-week institute the summer before they began implementing their new educational strategy, which included the adoption of Expeditionary Learning/Outward Bound. The costs for this summer institute were lower than one might guess, however. Because this was a reconstituted school with an entirely new staff, the school was able to make unpaid attendance of the institute a condition of hire for the new staff, bringing the costs down considerably. They also followed that intensive level of training with continued training, provided by an external school design team, during the school year.

In addition, several of the schools we studied hired initially one and then an additional half- or full-time individual, both of whom devoted their time to instructional leadership at the school. These schools considered these individuals permanent, on-site coaches who were there to provide the kind of in-classroom coaching and assistance that research shows is required for teachers to change their classroom practice (Joyce & Showers, 1998).

Thus, some of the schools we studied began to spend $100,000 to $150,000 per year for ongoing professional development, instructional leadership, and ongoing coaching. These are large amounts for schools with 500 students and represent far more than just marginal increases in training and professional development budgets. These stupendous investments are testimony to the importance these schools placed on enhancing the instructional expertise of their teachers. They believed that without this level of ongoing training, their restructuring efforts would not work. Chapter 5 shows how the schools found the money for these substantial investments.

School Size:
Creating Smaller High Schools

Finally, we address the issue of school size. The research is clear that small schools are more effective than large schools, that is, students in smaller schools learn more, other things being equal, than do students in larger schools. The positive achievement effects are even larger for low-income and minority students. Research shows that elementary schools should be between 300 and 500 students, and that between 600 and 900 students is the optimal size of high schools (Lee & Smith, 1997; Fowler & Walberg, 1991; Howley, 1989; Raywid, 1997/1998).

Most elementary schools fall within the above size parameters, but most high schools in larger districts do not. Outside of rural areas, most high schools enroll many more than 1,000 students. And because of that, most high school buildings are large enough to handle 1,500, 2,000, 3,000, and even larger numbers of students.

But several new, restructured high schools are able to meet, if not beat, the achievement levels of schools within the above size parameters, even when located in large buildings with 2,000 to 3,000 students. How is this accomplished? By dividing the school into several semi- (if not actually) autonomous schools-within-a-school. The Talent Development Middle and Talent Development High Schools provide one of the best examples of this approach for breaking large high schools into smaller sizes.

In a secondary school built for 2,000 students, for example, the Talent Development approach would divide the school building into four separate and autonomous schools with 500 students each. Each school would have its own faculty (one-fourth of the faculty provided for the 2,000 students) and a separate principal. Moreover, each school would have a separate entrance to make it feel like a different school even though it was sharing space with three other schools located in the same building. This approach does not allow the existence of large buildings to be an insurmountable hurdle to providing small secondary schools. But it goes beyond creating semiautonomous schools within schools. It actually creates four independent schools located in the same building, each physically separated from the other in an important way.

Linda Darling-Hammond (1996) describes another approach to creating smaller secondary schools. Central Park East Secondary is a school of 450 students located on the Upper East Side of Manhattan, close to East Harlem. Sixty percent of the students are eligible for free or reduced-price lunch, and 25% are eligible for some type of special education services. It receives the same per-pupil school funding as all other high schools in the city. Central Park East is able to offer a more intimate learning environment by virtue of its smaller size. But it goes further than that: It also groups those students into classes that average only 18 students, and each teacher sees only 36 students per week. It accomplishes this strategy by delivering the curriculum through integrated curriculum units of mathematics-science and English–social studies. It represents one of dozens of new, small secondary schools that have been created in New York City over the past decade.

Finally, we should note that Edison Secondary Academies are designed for only about 500 students each, and that nearly all of the emerging national secondary school designs also recommend an optimum size of 500 students (Comer, Haynes, Joyner, & Ben-Avie, 1996; Finnan, St. John, McCarthy, & Slovacek, 1996; Hirsch, 1996; Sizer, 1996; Stringfield et al.,

1996). In short, there are several proposals for and examples of new secondary schools that provide an instructional environment of fewer than 900 students, and closer to 500 students.

Summary

The many schools that have been studied have taken a variety of approaches to the issues of school and class size, student grouping, provision of time for planning and professional development, and resource expenditure for the type of intensive professional development that produces changes in classroom practice and results in higher levels of student learning. All of these structural approaches are driven by the overall educational strategy of the school. And whereas in the traditional education world, many of these structural approaches would require more money, in the schools studied, they were financed almost entirely with creative use of the funds that the school received from the normal school budget process.

Before describing how the schools reallocated resources to fund these structural changes, we first discuss in Chapter 4 their equally extensive strategies for serving students with special needs.

CHAPTER FOUR

Step 4:

Deciding How to Serve Students Who Need Extra Help

We have referred several times to the various strategies that schools selected to provide the extra help that some students need to learn to higher performance standards in the regular curriculum program. In these discussions, and in this chapter, we are not addressing the more complex service needs of students with severe or multiple disabilities. Instead, our focus, and the topic of discussion in this chapter, is that group of students of normal intelligence who, with extra help, can learn to the standards expected of all students. Such students include those with various mild disabilities, specific learning disabilities, the slower learner, students from low-income backgrounds, and students whose native language is not English. All of these students must put in extra effort as they struggle to learn to the higher and more difficult performance standards that are part of most schools', districts', and states' standards-based education reform agendas.

Whatever the school's overall educational strategy, it also needs an explicit strategy for struggling students to ensure that these students receive the extra help they need to perform to proficiency standards. Moreover, such a strategy entails more than a rhetorical claim, such as "We provide an inclusive approach." A school might implement an inclusionary approach, but many of the included struggling students might still require extra help (Fuchs & Fuchs, 1994-1995). In other words, inclusion per se is often insufficient; something extra for some students might also be required.

For example, the Modern Red Schoolhouse (Stringfield et al., 1996; http://www.mrsh.org) has adopted an inclusion policy for its struggling students. Such students are included in all regular classroom activities and must meet the same expectations as all other students. The descriptive materials for that comprehensive school design are very clear about the design's approach to the category of students that we refer to as struggling. However, the design does more than just include such students. Modern Red encourages schools to provide some type of individual, one-to-one tutoring for those students. So, if a school adopts the Modern Red design for its overall education strategy, it also needs to implement a tutoring strategy in order to fully provide all of the services required for its struggling students to learn to the level of the Modern Red curriculum standards.

Funding Resources
for Struggling Students

Before describing how the schools redesigned their strategies for struggling students, we first make some contextual comments about the funding resources that exist for providing the extra help that struggling students need. The fact is that all schools studied had considerable additional resources for a variety of special student needs. Indeed, during the past 30 to 35 years, the federal government and most states have developed numerous programs for special needs students and allocated dollars to fund those programs (Odden & Picus, 2000). Although it could be argued that no programs for special student needs are fully funded, the fact remains that large numbers of dollars have been provided through a variety of programs in recognition of the additional educational needs of many students.

Furthermore, programs for special needs students have garnered the lion's share of the new dollars that have been allocated to public schools over the past three decades. Rothstein and Miles (1995) studied the resource increase and resource allocation practices in nine districts over a

24-year time period and found that 38% of new revenues were spent on programs for special needs students, including special education, bilingual education, compensatory education, and desegregation. In a study of funding for special education, Lankford and Wyckoff (1995) found that this category alone nearly tripled in expenditure over a 12-year period and accounted for 85% of education dollar increases in New York. Odden and Picus (2000) show that in addition to the numerous federal programs for special needs students, most states also have a comprehensive array of such programs, all with considerable funding. In short, funding for students who must struggle harder to learn to high standards constitutes a significant portion of the overall education budget, and often a considerable portion of the budget of an individual school.

At the same time, there has been widespread disappointment with the effectiveness of the educational strategies that have been deployed with these considerable resources. For at least the past 15 years, studies of the effectiveness of bilingual education, programs supported under the Federal Title I and similar state compensatory education programs, as well as programs for students with disabilities have found that educational effects have been meager (e.g., Odden, 1991; Reynolds & Wolfe, 1999; Slavin, Karweit, & Madden, 1989; Vinovskis, 1999).

As mentioned a number of times in previous chapters, these were also the conclusions of the schools engaged in resource reallocation. Most had considerable numbers of students struggling to learn to higher standards and funds from several state and federal sources to help those students succeed. But every school studied had become disenchanted with the traditional strategies they had been employing. In general, the traditional strategies included some version of service in a resource room, which usually focused on remedial reading or mathematics. When students were provided extra help in their regular classroom, an instructional aide, rather than a licensed teacher, usually provided it. In a few cases, students had access to computerized instruction of basic skills. But in no case were the schools pleased with the achievement results. The students who needed the extra help were those who were served, but the service strategies had little to no effect on the academic learning of the students. All schools identified this as a major problem, and redesigning the services for struggling students became a central element of the restructuring and resource reallocation processes.

More Powerful Strategies
for Struggling Students

The schools studied adopted two new ways to address the needs of struggling students. Both were costly, and both were funded by reallocating the resources that previously had funded the strategies the schools decided to drop. The two new strategies were the following:

► One-to-one tutoring, ideally provided by a licensed teacher

► Class sizes of close to 15, ideally taught by a dual licensed teacher

Research shows that one-to-one tutoring is the most effective educational strategy for helping young students learn to read (Wasik & Slavin, 1993). Armed with this knowledge, many of the elementary schools studied reallocated resources away from their traditional remedial reading strategies to the support of teacher tutors who worked with students on an individual basis. In most cases, a teacher would spend about 20 minutes a day with each of 12 to 15 students, providing them with one-to-one tutoring in reading. Furthermore, it was the students in grades 1-3 who received the vast bulk of the tutoring service.

An important question to answer when trying to determine the costs of such a strategy is, How many tutors does a school need? Although there is no definitive answer to this question, the Success for All program has provided some guidelines. Until recently, that program suggested that a school of 500 students should have one tutor for every 25% of its students eligible for free and reduced-price lunch; this also was the tutoring number suggested by the New American Schools for the more comprehensive Roots and Wings version of this educational strategy (Odden, 1997a). Following these guidelines, every school of 500 would have at least one tutor, and an all-poverty school would have four tutors.

More recently, the Success for All web page (http://www.successforall.net) suggests that a school of 500 students should seek to have one tutor for every 20% of students from low-income family backgrounds, usually measured by student eligibility for free and reduced-price lunch. This is the tutoring level that is now provided to schools in New Jersey that are the target of that state's major school finance court decision, which requires schools to adopt a whole school reform model and fund it through resource reallocation. In identifying the cost resources required for each whole school design, the state suggests a budget category of five teacher tutor positions (Analt et al., 1999).

Robert Slavin, the founder of Success for All, has been quoted as saying that if schools want to produce a much larger percentage of students reading proficiently by the third grade, then a tutoring strategy at the levels noted above would be adequate. This would produce "success for most." But he has also said that depending on the specific needs of the school, if it really wanted "success for all," it might need to hire even more tutors.

Houston has done just that. In addition to implementing the Success for All program in about 80 of its elementary schools, which includes teacher tutors, the district has developed an additional tutoring strategy for students who are still struggling in grades 4-6. The upper-grade tutors are trained instructional assistants and not fully licensed teachers. But the district follows the procedure developed by George Farkas (1998, 1999), who has designed an effective instructional-aide-as-tutor program. Every aide serving as a tutor must meet a stringent literacy requirement, that is, he or she must be educated and literate, and then must undergo a multiple-week training program in a specific tutoring curriculum. These para-professional tutors are then closely supervised while they are tutoring the upper-elementary-grade students.

Thus, to deploy an extensive tutoring strategy, a school of 500 students could have up to five or more licensed teacher tutors for students in grades 1-3, and several other paraprofessional, trained tutors for grades 4-6. It should be clear that such a strategy for struggling students would be quite powerful, but also quite expensive.

None of the schools we studied implemented this kind of intensive tutoring strategy, and several used instructional assistants for tutoring even grade 1-3 students. Thus, many schools did not completely follow the guidelines of the Success for All program. Nevertheless, they all had begun the process of dismantling their previous ineffective strategies for serving struggling students and were phasing in a more intensive, research-based tutoring strategy.

The second new strategy for serving struggling students was to reduce class sizes to the 15- to 17-student range. As mentioned previously, many of these schools had commonsense rationales that smaller class sizes would be better, particularly for special needs students, and could point to the positive results from the Tennessee class size reduction experiment. This study showed that small classes of around 15 students for K-3, in and of themselves, were associated with improvements in student learning. The study also showed that the learning gains were about twice that for low-income and minority students, often the characteristics of students in the variety of special needs programs (Grissmer, 1999). Furthermore, the study showed that these learning gains persisted into middle and high school (Finn & Achilles, 1999). Thus, several schools around the country have been adopting a small class size strategy as a more powerful way to serve not only all students, but also students with special needs (see also Achilles, 1999).

This strategy is also expensive. For example, consider a school with 500 students. At class sizes of 25, the school needs 20 teachers (plus an additional 20%, or four teachers, to provide planning and preparation time for those teachers). If it reduced class sizes to 17 for all grades, it would need 30 teachers, which means 10 additional teachers. If it reduced class sizes to 17 just for grades 1-3, it would need five extra teachers.

Note that the class size reduction strategy for just grades 1-3 requires about the same number of additional teachers as the basic tutoring strategy: an extra five teaching positions. Although none of the schools we studied viewed these two different approaches as alternative ways to use five additional teaching positions, analytically, that is the case. This is the sort of thinking in which schools need to engage in order to ensure that they are spending their resources as effectively as possible.

One of the questions usually asked about the class size reduction strategy is whether there is enough classroom space for such a strategy. We addressed this issue in Chapter 3. But for places that do not have the space, there is some evidence that two teachers in one class of 30 can also have a positive impact, although the impact is not the same as two different classes of just 15 students (Molnar et al., 1999). We would caution schools about this two-teacher strategy because other reports have concluded that such a strategy does not produce the expected result. Furthermore, the Tennessee class size reduction strategy also showed that adding an instructional aide to a regular classroom had little impact (Achilles, 1999). Nevertheless, it might be possible to implement the two-teacher strategy in schools without additional classroom space in a way that does produce a significant educational impact on students, so it remains an option for schools.

Many schools augmented either or both of the above strategies with an additional requirement that teachers have two areas of licensure. This strategy was used in nearly all schools that we studied that reduced class size, and it appeared in some schools that implemented a tutoring program as well. The idea was that if the struggling students were to be given extra help by the regular teacher, the teacher needed a broader array of expertise in addition to the fewer number of students in the small class. As mentioned earlier, some schools required a second license in ESL, others in learning disabilities, and some in reading, depending on the particular needs of their student population.

As a result, most of the schools studied provided struggling students with a combination of new strategies:

▶ First, a better and more rigorous curriculum, with expectations that all struggling students would be taught that curriculum and would learn the material along with the other students

▶ Second, either instruction in a much smaller class so that they could receive additional help from their regular teacher, or individual one-to-one tutoring so that they could receive intensive assistance if they began to fall behind

▶ Third, often both regular and additional instruction from teachers who had expertise directly linked to the educational issues with which the student was struggling

In short, the new strategies for struggling students were multiple in their dimension and were based on research that implied they would be more powerful as well.

We should also say that because many teacher tutors taught a regular reading class in most Success for All schools, struggling students in those schools had the additional advantage of receiving their reading instruction in small classes. Thus, they actually received four different aspects of a new strategy for struggling students: a more rigorous reading curriculum, instruction in a small class, instruction from a more skilled teacher, and tutoring if they fell behind. Such an intensive and comprehensive strategy should produce greater learning effects for those struggling students.

When education reformers are all focused on raising the achievement levels of all students, major reforms such as these can be accomplished. A further example helps illustrate that it may be possible for large numbers of schools across the country to provide all four of these strategies simply by using current dollars differently. One of the schools we studied (a K-2 school) that reallocated resources to reduce class sizes to 15, is located in a district that decided to implement the same strategy for all of its elementary schools beginning in the fall of 2000. A task force had recommended that the district reduce class sizes to 15 in grades 1-3 for all schools with a student poverty concentration of 40% or higher. After fiscal and space analysis, the district decided it had the resources to do so, using just state equalization and local property tax funds. Over a 3-month period, it devised a strategy to do so that was to be implemented for the 2000-2001 school year.

But in late fall 1999, its state legislature expanded a state program that was also designed to reduce class sizes to 15 in grades 1-3. So, beginning in the fall of 2000, the state will provide the dollars to accomplish that class size reduction policy—reduce class sizes to 15 in grades 1-3 for all schools with 40% or more of their students eligible for free and reduced-price lunch. Now the district must decide the following:

1. What should it do with the local funds that would have been used to reduce class size if the state program had not financed the project?

2. What should it do with its reading curriculum to ensure that the new class size reduction policy will be complemented with an appropriate and effective reading program?

3. How should it encourage schools to use their Title I funds differently now that students will be instructed in small classes?

We suggest that the district use its extra funds and encourage schools to use their Title I funds to hire teacher tutors in order to maximize the possibility that all students will learn to read proficiently by grade 3. This strategy will work most effectively in combination with a strong reading curriculum and small classes. We would hope that elementary schools in this district would eliminate both remedial pull-out teachers and diminish, if not abolish, the practice of using nonlicensed teacher aides to instruct struggling students in reading. In short, we hope that the district takes the next step in reallocating resources to provide tutoring services, now that the state has provided the extra money to reduce class sizes. Implementing both of these strategies for helping struggling students learn to read, only one of which was possible for most of the schools we studied, should be even more powerful than implementing only one of them. This is an example of the kinds of broad changes that can be made when additional funds are available.

Secondary schools also need strategies for struggling students. Although the research is less clear on what the best policies are, the first step is to require all students—regardless of their achievement level entering high school—to take a rigorous set of academic courses, including algebra in the ninth grade instead of general mathematics. Research is clear that a rigorous set of academic courses is the prime prerequisite for higher levels of high school learning, even for slower achievers and those who enter high school far behind academically (Gamoran, Porter, Smithson, & White, 1997; Lee, Bryk, & Smith, 1993; Lee & Smith, 1997; Odden, 1997c).

Another strategy is to rethink the use of electives, particularly those that are nonacademic. For example, the Talent Development Middle School and the Talent Development High School, a secondary school strategy to which we have referred several times, deploys an "elective replacement" strategy for students struggling with academics. Rather than a nonacademic elective, these students take an additional period of mathematics, science, or whatever class they are struggling in. This strategy gives a clear priority to academics and provides extra academic services, again at no extra cost.

The High Schools That Work school design (http://www.sreb.org/Programs/hstw/high.html) has tried to completely rethink traditional career-oriented electives. This secondary school design was created explicitly for students who had traditionally not done well in high school. This high school strategy has not only redesigned all career- and vocationally oriented courses to include academics, but also requires a core set of academic courses throughout a student's high school career. Research shows the program to be one of the few high school designs that produces improved student performance (Herman, 1999; Traub, 1999).

In addition, middle and high schools across the country are expanding after-school, weekend, and summer school programs to provide struggling students with the extra time needed to boost their achievement to acceptable performance standards. The Talent Development schools are an example of schools that offer these strategies. In some cases, these offerings require extra money, but most states fund summer school if it has an academic focus and is required for a student's academic program. Although the research is mixed on some of these extra time strategies, mainly because the academic focus in these programs in the past has often been weak, the effects should be much larger if the instruction is standards based and provides the extra time that struggling secondary students need to boost their performance.

Some Resource-Room
Services Remain

Even with all of these changes to strategies for serving special needs students, all of the schools we studied retained some level of resource-room service. Resource rooms were often used for emotionally disturbed students who, although mainstreamed most of the day, had to have a place to go if they could not handle the regular classroom environment. Other times, resource rooms were used to provide extra help in mathematics, or the extra help needed by students in grades 4-6. Even the rural K-8 school that reduced class sizes to approximately 17 and enacted the dual licensure strategy (with the second license in learning disabilities) retained two resource rooms for students with more intractable educational challenges.

Although this practice might suggest that the schools hedged in their restructuring and resource reallocation agendas, it also shows the wisdom of schools in not completely "betting the bank" on a new strategy. Although bold, the schools were also cautious. They had concluded that most students would learn more in small classes or with some individual tutoring, but they also knew that some more traditional strategies would still be necessary. In this way, schools combined new initiatives that studies have begun to prove more effective with some elements of the old strategy. They did this with the rationale that the former strategies were not completely flawed and served some purposes for which students still had needs.

Changing Individual
Education Programs

Many students struggling to meet the standards of a curriculum have an Individual Education Program (IEP). All students who receive such special education services under federal and state programs for the disabled are required to have an IEP. The IEP emerges from an intensive assessment and evaluation of the students' learning needs and specifies the type and nature of extra services that they should receive. Developing and approving each student's IEP is a process subject to legal review in order to ensure that the needs of the student are met.

Therefore, if the strategy for serving a student with special needs is changed, his or her IEP must also be changed in order to make the new strategy legal. This law serves an important purpose. It requires schools to assess whether the changes they are making will hinder the special-needs student's ability to learn—a crucial consideration for any school making changes to the delivery of its educational program. Chapter 5 shows that the largest portion of dollars that schools reallocated derived from funding for special needs programs, so the issue of the IEP is of critical importance to this discussion.

All of the schools that we studied changed the IEPs for all of the special education students whose delivery of services changed as a result of the program restructuring activities. All schools stated that this required a great deal of effort because the new IEP had to be explained to each student's parents or legal guardians, and the process for modifying the IEP had to be followed faithfully. However, some faculties said that there had been an unacceptable degree of laxity in both the development and use of IEPs before the school restructuring. Therefore, the faculties believed that the new service strategies would be more effective and serve the students better, and in the process of implementing those strategies, they also improved the IEPs for all students who needed them.

We know of, but did not study, one school in a midwestern state that reallocated a variety of categorical program resources for smaller class sizes for all students all day long, just as the other two schools did that we studied in that same state. But the former school did not seek program waivers nor change student IEPs as part of its restructuring, whereas the latter two did. And not surprisingly, the former had to reverse its restructuring under state order, whereas the latter two received waivers and were in compliance with all IEP requirements.

The lesson here is that neither program restructuring nor resource reallocation, no matter how powerful the new strategy, can proceed without regard to the needs of special students and legalities within the current system. The corollary lesson is that permission often will be granted to make changes that have an educational rationale, and that even IEPs can and need to be changed to reflect the new way of providing extra services to special needs students. Although there have been regulatory excesses in the past, the rules were designed to ensure that students' needs are served. Some of those rules can be bent if a new service strategy has a sound educational justification and if all of the parties (teachers, parents, etc.) approve the new service strategy in the student's revised IEP.

Encouragement From Both Federal and State Governments

Rethinking the provision of services for special needs students, particularly services paid for by federal Title I, bilingual, special education, and similar categorical programs, is something that is actively encouraged by the U.S. Department of Education, as well as the U.S. Congress. As mentioned previously, the federal government changed the regulations for Title I in 1995 to allow schools with 50% or more of their students from low-income backgrounds to use Title I funds for schoolwide programs. This regulatory change emerged because of disenchantment with the traditional pull-out approach to providing Title I services. The thought was that a schoolwide program with a rigorous curriculum program at its core would be more effective than pull-out instruction in remedial mathematics and reading, the all-too-typical traditional use of Title I funds.

The federal government's encouragement of more cohesive programs is also reflected in a 1990s provision that formally allows districts and schools to merge funds from nearly a dozen categorical programs and apply them to standards-based, schoolwide efforts. Finally, the Comprehensive School Reform program, enacted in 1998, provides small grants for up to 3 years to schools adopting or designing schoolwide efforts, the bulk of which are funded by resource reallocation of both state and federal categorical program funds.

Thus, the stimulus for altering strategies for struggling students that we and others observed are reinforced by new formal and informal policies of both federal and state education agencies. These policies encourage schools to rethink their efforts to serve struggling students and to redesign those efforts to include a more rigorous set of expectations and new services that are more effective in actually producing the achievement levels that meet those standards.

Support From Unions

One implementation issue for both of the above new strategies for educating struggling students is whether the strategy is supported or opposed by the local teacher union. Whether schools implement a smaller class size or tutoring strategy, they are eliminating some teacher roles within the school and creating new ones. Those teachers with the eliminated roles could possibly resist and even ask their union to protect their previous positions.

This phenomenon emerged in nearly all of the schools studied. But those schools that worked with the union to ease the transition and to place teachers whose positions were eliminated in similar positions in other schools had more success in fully implementing their new approaches than did the schools that did not make such efforts. For example, we studied one school that reduced class sizes to 15 by eliminating four pull-out ESL and Title I positions. All of these teachers took the issue to their union, which happened to be a very traditional union that had not actively embraced the district's standards-based reform agenda. Most people in the district expected strong opposition from the union. But that did not happen to the extent that some had feared it would. The union wrote a letter to the school board seeking clarification of the school change and requested that the teachers receive a similar role in another school. It then let the restructuring school's strategy stand, in part because it was teacher developed and supported by all of the other teachers at the site.

Summary

As the details of resource reallocation are described in the next chapter, readers would be wise to translate the dollar changes into personnel changes to begin to understand the types of changes that these schools are making. Because so many teacher positions are affected in most schools' resource reallocation efforts, attention has to be given to the personal and political aspects of these changes. And the teacher's union needs to be involved in the process. Although this involvement might slow progress in the very short term, it likely will help speed progress in the medium to long term. Opposition from an uninvolved union could well doom such change in the short term, so schools and their districts will need to garner passive or active union support if program and resource allocation changes are to move forward.

CHAPTER FIVE

Step 5:

Paying for the Changes

In this book thus far, we have discussed the many new strategies that schools are adopting in an effort to improve student achievement, and we have made reference to the fact that many have done so via resource reallocation. In the previous two chapters, we showed how the choices about which educational strategies to adopt help schools decide which resources to reallocate. But we have not fully delved into the details about which dollars were reallocated at the schools studied. In this chapter, we begin by looking across sites to come up with the major sources of resource reallocation at both district and school levels. In doing so, we also give specific examples of how schools reallocated resources to pay for their new educational strategies.

Resource Reallocation at the District Level

Although one could think about resource reallocation at the district level as potentially including some of the resources that districts allocate to schools, this section discusses only the potential for reallocation of district resources spent on central functions. Central offices appear large because they house the operation and maintenance functions, the transportation and food systems, and the business office, and also provide instructional support. Together, these functions can comprise 25% of the overall operating budget of a district. But central office *administrative* expenditures, which many people believe to be quite large and therefore see this area as ripe for resource reallocation, tend to average only 3% to 4% of the entire district budget, and surprisingly, even a smaller percentage in the largest districts (Odden, Monk, Nakib, & Picus, 1995). Therefore, even when these expenditures can be reduced, they will not provide substantial extra money. Furthermore, although efficiencies can be found in operations, maintenance, transportation, and food services, those additional dollars are also limited.

Nevertheless, there is potential for central office resource reallocation sufficient to fund an intensive professional development strategy. A good example of this approach is Community District 2 in New York City (Elmore & Burney, 1996). That central office expanded professional development dramatically by eliminating most of the categorical program and instructional support staff and turning the funds supporting those positions into dollars for professional development. The district eliminated nearly all district-level program support staff for federal (Title I) and state compensatory education programs and bilingual education, and it reduced the amount of money used for special education program support. It took those funds and reallocated them to professional development focused on reading, writing, and mathematics. Over a 5-year period, the district expanded professional development expenditures to about 5% of its operating budget. It then used those funds to focus relentlessly on developing teachers' instructional expertise in reading. After that time period, the district's students produced one of the highest-ever scores on the New Standards Reference assessments.

The superintendent in charge of the overhaul of District 2, Anthony Alvarado, is currently the Chancellor for Instruction in San Diego. One of his first actions (with the superintendent) in that district was to reduce that central office by about 10% to begin the process of reallocating a large portion of the operating budget for a similar kind of focused, intensive, and ongoing professional development in literacy and numeracy.

In sum, there is potential at the central office to reallocate staffing resources and other central resources. It may not represent a large percentage of the total district budget that can be reallocated, but it is important

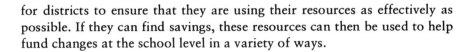

for districts to ensure that they are using their resources as effectively as possible. If they can find savings, these resources can then be used to help fund changes at the school level in a variety of ways.

Resource Reallocation at the School Level

Most of any district's budget is spent at the school site. Instructional expenditures constitute about 60% of most districts' budgets; these expenditures include regular instruction and instruction for the wide variety of categorical programs for special needs students. Site administration represents another 3% to 5%. In total, at least 80% of most districts' budgets are spent at and within school sites for a variety of services provided directly to students (see Odden et al., 1995). Thus, the site budget should be the primary focus for resource reallocation because it includes the largest portion of the overall district budget.

Of the funds spent at the school site, the majority is spent on personnel. Often, this fact is a barrier to many faculties understanding the possibilities for reallocating these dollars. Staff are seen as a given, and only nonstaff dollars are considered for reallocation. This is especially true for schools that are still staffed by the central office, but research has shown that it often remains true for schools who gain control over their budgets as well (Odden et al., 1999).

But this psychological constraint to envisioning the wide range of possibilities for different use of school resources, primarily site staffing resources, can be diminished by actions that allow sites to view school resources as more discretionary. One of the best examples for encouraging this perspective has been the change in requirements for spending federal Title I dollars.

In many of the schools studied, Title I, the federal compensatory education program, was increasingly being viewed as a discretionary pot of money. This was partially due to the fact that many of these schools served a large number of students from low-income backgrounds. Because more than 50% of the students from most of these schools were from low-income backgrounds, as measured by eligibility for free or reduced-price lunch, the schools were eligible to spend their Title I funds for schoolwide programs. Furthermore, at one of the schools we studied where the percentage of students in poverty fell below the 50% threshold, the principal applied for and received a waiver to use all Title I dollars for a schoolwide program.

Thus, in many schools, Title I funds began to represent a fairly large sum of money, formerly targeted to programs just for low-income students, that schools could now apply to virtually any program that was used throughout the school. The desire to use these funds for schoolwide programs was intensified at many schools by their dissatisfaction with the effects of the Title I-supported pull-out programs that they had in place to serve low-income students. Indeed, the effectiveness of traditional pull-out programs and use of instructional aides, the former dominant use of Title I dollars, is being questioned by both researchers (Borman & D'Agostino, 1996; Vinovskis, 1999) and many of the practitioners at the various school sites studied.

Although the ability to use Title I dollars differently was often the initial catalyst that stimulated schools to think about program change and resource reallocation, as they did so, they often came to realize that the entire school budget, particularly all of the staffing in the school, could potentially be reallocated. In other words, it was not just the staffing and strategies for Title I services that could be questioned in their effectiveness, but also the staffing and resources used for nearly all other school services as well.

In order to analyze the staffing changes that were made and the resources that were reallocated in the schools studied, it is useful to think of a school's staff as being divided among six categories:

1. *Classroom teachers:* Teachers who teach the core curriculum to students for most of each day. The core curriculum is usually defined as reading, writing, language arts, mathematics, science, social studies, and, in secondary schools, foreign language.

2. *Regular education specialists:* Teachers of subjects outside the core curriculum, such as art, physical education, library, and music, who also provide planning and preparation time for classroom teachers. In secondary schools, this can also include staff who provide electives such as vocational, business, family and home, and consumer education.

3. *Categorical program specialists:* Teachers outside the regular education classroom whose salaries are paid largely by categorical program dollars, including special education, compensatory education (Title I), bilingual/ESL, gifted and talented, and other programs for special needs students.

4. *Pupil support specialists:* Professional staff who provide non-academic support services to students outside the regular education classroom, such as guidance counselors, psychologists, and nurses.

5. *Aides:* Paraprofessional staff who provide either instructional support (including working one-on-one with children both within the regular classroom and in resource rooms) or noninstructional support (including clerical tasks and supervising the cafeteria and/or playground).

6. *Other Staff:* Any other staff employed by the school, including clerical, cafeteria, and custodial workers.

Although different schoolwide educational strategies require schools to reallocate different combinations of staff, the paragraphs that follow use these six staffing categories to discuss the resource and staffing reallocations made at the schools studied. Because these staffing categories are all linked to funding sources, these paragraphs will also detail which funding sources were tapped as schools reallocated resources to their new educational strategies.

Classroom Teachers

The first category, classroom teachers, represents the largest staff category in most schools. Most of the funding for regular classroom teachers derives from local and state equalization aid dollars. For some of the schools in our study, those dollars arrive at the school in a lump sum to be spent as the school sees fit. Of course, many districts have class size maximums that dictate the minimum number of classroom teachers they must hire.

For numerous reasons, schools rarely tapped this staffing category for reallocation. A number of schools, including both elementary and high schools, actually increased the number of classroom teachers in order to reduce class size, usually far below the maximum levels. Indeed, several elementary schools pooled resources from nearly all other staffing categories to support a strategy of reducing class sizes to between 15 and 17 students all day long (Odden & Archibald, in press; or see http://www.wcer.wisc.edu/cpre).

As discussed in Chapter 3, Miles and Darling-Hammond (1998) studied high schools that did the same thing, providing class sizes of about 18. By also implementing an integrated curriculum strategy, these high schools reduced the teacher-student contact to just 36 students per day (compared to the typical 150 in most large high schools), thus making the learning environment more personal and potentially more effective.

We have studied four elementary schools that essentially took all of the resources from other staffing categories and, like the successful schools in the East Austin, Texas case (Murnane & Levy, 1996), used them to hire additional teachers to reduce class sizes to the low range of 15 to 17 students. One school in a rural district took this approach. It transformed four teachers who had been working in pull-out resource rooms and who had dual certification in regular and special education into classroom teachers and used the salaries of four instructional aide positions to hire two additional classroom teachers. Thus, the school was able to reduce class sizes to 17. Another school in a medium-sized urban district took the funds from three positions that had supported ESL teachers in a pull-out format, and together with funds from Title I, gifted and talented, and some discretionary local sources, hired four more teachers and reduced overall class sizes to 17. In a larger urban district in the east, we studied two elementary schools that implemented a variation of these approaches, all for the purpose of reducing class size to the 15 to 17 range.

At the same time, we studied two elementary schools that allowed class sizes to increase somewhat in order to allow them to fund professional teacher tutors and full-time instructional facilitators. These schools believed that it was more important to have somewhat larger classes (27 to 28 students) augmented by the intensive help provided by teacher tutors, rather than smaller classes (22 to 24 students) without any tutoring help. The schools' faculties decided that the small negatives from the modest increases in class size were offset by the large positives of hiring tutors and providing substantially more professional development and coaching.

Both of these schools had adopted the Success for All reading program and were strongly committed to the tutoring, professional development, and instructional leadership that was part of that educational strategy. By choosing to fund tutors and an instructional facilitator rather than hire additional classroom teachers to maintain class sizes at 25 or lower, these schools effectively reallocated resources away from traditional regular education expenditures.

Miles and Darling-Hammond (1998) found this same phenomenon for two schools that also had adopted the Success for All program; the schools' faculty decided that the small negatives from the modest increases in class size were offset by the large benefits of hiring tutors and a full-time instructional facilitator.

Barring these examples, the staffing category of classroom teachers was generally not tapped as a source for resource reallocation. In most cases, if there was any change to the resources allocated to regular classroom teacher positions, it was in the direction of additional resources.

Regular Education Specialists

Staffing resources for regular education specialists generally were not reduced either. Like regular education classroom teachers, the funding source for this category is local and state equalization aid dollars. The reasons for not reallocating these resources were twofold. First, these schools valued the subject matter that these specialists taught, and they believed, for the most part, that these subjects required specialists and could not be covered as thoroughly by incorporating them into the regular education classroom. Second, the teacher contract usually required planning and preparation time for classroom teachers, and the regular education specialists provided this time. Thus, regular education specialists were viewed as necessary for fulfilling contractual obligations.

However, as discussed previously, schools found numerous ways to provide teachers with the time they needed to prepare for and engage in the program restructuring required to implement their educational visions. A few of these strategies did not require keeping the same number of special-ist teachers to provide planning time. For example, a school could decide to organize some special classes, such as physical education, into larger classes than those taught by classroom teachers, thus allowing one specialist to provide planning time for more than one teacher during a single class peri-od. Employing such a strategy freed up the funding that had supported spe-cialists without reducing planning time and, one could argue, without com-promising student achievement in the core subjects.

Another school modestly increased the staff in this area, as well as changed the subjects that were taught. Most interestingly, this school replaced an art teacher (a subject that they believed could be integrated into the regular education classroom) with a teacher of social skills (a subject they wanted taught to the large numbers of students from poverty back-grounds). Chapter 3 also discusses the school that sought to turn several full-time specialist positions into several more part-time specialist teachers, thus stretching the number of teachers and blocks of collaborative planning time that the funds for these positions could support.

In sum, although planning and preparation time for teachers is impor-tant, it may be possible to provide this time more efficiently than is tradi-tionally done at most schools. However, for the most part, we found that when specialist teachers were part of a school budget, they tended to remain part of a school budget. The only exceptions were when schools created a more efficient strategy to provide the same amount of planning and preparation time for classroom teachers with a different specialist teacher strategy, such as the two discussed.

Categorical Program Specialists

The most extensive resource reallocations were within the area of cate-gorical program specialists. There are many reasons for this phenomenon, but simply stated, this is the area where schools had the most discretionary money and were most unhappy with the results of the strategies they had been deploying. There are three primary funding sources for this staffing category: (a) compensatory education funding for remedial and resource-room specialists who provide assistance to low-income students; (b) special education funds, which pay for the specialists who provide services both

within and outside the regular classroom for students with disabilities; and
(c) ESL funds for students who need to learn English.

Compensatory education. Although compensatory education dollars
derive from local, state, and federal sources, for most schools, the largest
source of funding comes from the federal Title I program. In percentage
terms, Title I represented approximately 10% of the total budget at two of
the schools we studied.

All five schools in one study (Odden & Archibald, in press) were able
to apply Title I funds to schoolwide programs, but they used their funds in
different ways. Three schools used the resources to deploy tutors and
instructional facilitators, and to pay for the professional development that
was part of the Success for All design. One school used the resources to
help hire more classroom teachers to keep class sizes down. For these four
schools, as well as for other schools engaging in resource reallocation
around the country, federal compensatory education resources were instru-
mental in enabling them to implement their reforms.

Schools are also beginning to alter the use of funds from state pupil
weights for students eligible for free or reduced-price lunch and/or who
are Title I eligible, which have amounted to large sums in Minnesota and
Illinois. One Minnesota school we studied received almost $1,000 for each
student from a poverty background. In the year we studied it, the school
was given control over those funds and decided to eliminate two child
development specialists and fund tutors and an instructional facilitator
instead.

Although it is not true of all schools, in some schools, the level of federal and state compensatory education dollars is sufficient that, when reallocated, it can fund a range of expensive new educational strategies, such as
those included in the comprehensive Roots and Wings school design. For
an all low-income school of about 500 students, this design roughly
requires two instructional facilitators (one for reading and one for mathematics), four teacher tutors, a family liaison, and $70,000 for materials and
training. In large numbers of schools, reallocated Title I funds covered the
bulk of these additional costs. In the schools studied, additional resources
came from the reallocation of remedial reading and math resource room
teachers and instructional aides for the more effective elements listed
above.

Special education. For most of the schools implementing one of the educational strategies that we have described here, resources for special education constituted the second largest source of categorical staffing resources that were reallocated. Special education dollars, which derive from local, state, and federal sources, often fund staff in pull-out resource rooms for students with mental or physical disabilities. Many disabled students require services outside the regular classroom, but some, especially those with mild learning disabilities, can be better served in the regular education classroom. If the decision is made to integrate some of these students into the regular classroom, the funding for the services that are no longer provided outside the regular classroom can be reallocated.

At one rural school that implemented an inclusionary model with reduced class sizes, almost all of the money formerly spent on pull-out programs for special education was reallocated. Five special education teachers who were dual certified in special education and regular education were reassigned to regular education classrooms of their own in order to reduce class size. One other similarly dual-certified teacher was hired the year the school adopted the inclusionary model because of rising enrollment. In addition, four instructional aide positions were eliminated in order to hire two more dual-certified teachers. In total, eight dual-certified teachers took over regular classrooms in an effort to reduce class sizes from 25 to approximately 15, representing a substantial reallocation of special education resources. Later in the chapter, we discuss the waiver that the school had to obtain in order to implement this strategy.

At three other schools, a smaller portion of staffing formerly used for pull-out special education services was also used differently, again because of the overall education strategy, in this case the Success for All reading program. The Success for All reading program groups students by reading achievement levels. These three schools decided to have a special education teacher teach the reading class for the students who were having the most trouble with reading. In many cases, these teachers were dual certified in special education or remedial reading as well as regular education, so they were able to teach a homogeneous group of lower level readers more easily. The changes made to special education at these schools represent a reallocation of special education resources to the regular classroom. It should be noted that in order to make this reallocation legal, many students' individual education plans (IEPs) had to be changed to reflect the new methods by which they were being served.

English as a Second Language (ESL). Another source of categorical program dollars with potential for resource reallocation is ESL. Although this possibility applies only to schools with a significant number of students with limited English proficiency, schools that do have such students often get funding from a combination of local, state, and federal sources. Like compensatory education funds, these funds are often used for pull-out programs that are intended to raise student achievement levels. However, a school we studied with a high number of students with limited English proficiency questioned whether this was the most effective way of serving these students. How it chose to reallocate ESL resources and restructure services for those students is detailed in Chapter 6.

Pupil Support Specialists

Although pupil support specialists, who are funded by local dollars, do not amount to a very large share of a school's staffing budget, schools implementing new educational strategies have reallocated some resources from this category. These schools reconsidered how their resources were being allocated to fund pupil support and were able to find some money that could be used more effectively in other areas. For example, two schools chose to spend less money on a school nurse than the district suggested, thereby freeing up those resources for other purposes. Another school reallocated a half-time position from the guidance office to a half-time Reading Recovery teacher who was responsible for tutoring students who fell behind in reading. This provides yet another example of a reallocation of resources made to support research-based strategies for improving student achievement.

A high school studied by Miles and Darling-Hammond (1998) represents the boldest reallocation of pupil support staff. That school eliminated all pupil support specialists—guidance counselors, and so on—and embedded their functions into expanded roles for teachers. At this school, teachers spent 120 minutes each day with their homeroom class of 18 students. Over the school year, teachers were responsible for providing the guidance counseling, college advising, and nonacademic support that students needed, rather than having specialist staff to perform these functions. This school decided that by requiring these broader functions for teachers, but for only a small number of students, they were able to personalize these services, make them more effective, and free up some resources traditionally spent on pupil support staff.

Still, this was not a category from which a lot of resources were reallocated. In part, this is due to the fact that these positions represent a small part of the budget. The other reason we did not see a lot of reallocation away from this category might be because many of the schools' overall new education strategies did not have an element focused on this topic. For other schools, pupil support specialists already on staff fulfilled the roles required by the design they chose to implement. For example, schools that implemented Success for All, which has a family liaison position as part of its design, were able to use pupil support positions already on staff to cover those functions.

Aides

The existence and use of instructional aides is a vexing issue in most U.S. schools. On one hand, there is great demand from teachers for instructional aides. Indeed, in 1997, as districts in New Jersey received almost $1,000 per pupil in additional funding as part of the continuing implementation of that state's school finance decision, one of the goals in many districts was to provide each teacher with an instructional aide. North Carolina, for example, spends several hundred million dollars providing an instructional aide in every classroom for grades K-2.

But there is increasing evidence and understanding that instructional aides rarely add value in terms of increased student achievement. Thus, in a rising number of districts, instructional aide positions are being eliminated by the central office as part of restructuring and resource reallocation efforts. Pueblo, Colorado adopted this position, eliminating all instructional aide positions in 1997 and using the resources for reading specialists in schools. As a result of this change, reading performance rose dramatically in several of their schools (Sack, 1999). One school we studied adopted a version of the same policy; the superintendent eliminated all instructional aide positions over a summer, thus turning those dollars into discretionary dollars for each school. We should note that despite this district's attempt to force reallocation of these positions, many of the schools used those discretionary resources to hire back those aides.

Houston has probably taken one of the most sophisticated positions on the use of aides. First, it virtually eliminated all aide positions in grades K-3, as it implemented the Success for All reading program in most of its elementary schools. But, going beyond what even Success for All requires, it decided to implement a tutoring program for students in grades 4-6 to ensure that they maintained their reading capabilities. It used aides for this tutoring approach, but adopted the George Farkas (1998, 1999) strategy that we mentioned previously for deploying instructional aides as tutors. Each aide had to meet a high-level literacy test, each was given several weeks of training in a specific reading curriculum, and each was supervised closely as he or she engaged in his or her tutoring responsibilities.

We have also studied a charter school in Los Angeles that took a different approach to its aides. For the instructional aides, it adopted a knowledge and skills approach to their hourly wage: The more college credits they amassed, the higher their salary. The goal over time was to get every aide trained as a fully licensed teacher, thereby providing a career ladder for their instructional aides to develop into full-fledged, professional teachers. This school even paid the tuition for the courses the aides took.

In sum, resource reallocation of aides at the schools we and others have studied has generally meant reallocating or changing the role of instructional aides in the school, but retaining most noninstructional aides in order to have these personnel supervise the playground and cafeteria. One school eliminated four instructional aide positions in order to hire two additional regular education classroom teachers to reduce class size. In several other schools, the role of instructional aides was changed from that of general instructional support in the classroom to a one-on-one reading tutor. Although aides who are not specifically trained as reading tutors do not have the same impact on student performance as do regularly licensed teacher tutors (Shanahan, 1998), this change in the use of aides nevertheless represents a shift to using aides for research-supported functions like tutoring rather than as general classroom helpers.

Other Staff

The varied nature of school budgets makes it difficult to name all of the staff members who could potentially fall into an "other staff" category. For our purposes, it is necessary to mention only clerical and custodial staff. In fact, the main reason for including such a category here is to illustrate that although they do not comprise a large portion of the budget, the funds for clerical and custodial positions do represent a potential area for resource reallocation. At one Northwestern school, the administrator decided that the school could make do with four fewer hours of custodial time per week. Although this is not a significant amount of resources, it demonstrates how a school rethinking its current allocation can find ways to spend its money more effectively.

On the other hand, all of the schools in our study except one found it necessary to increase the amount of resources for clerical support. In some cases, the staff attributed the increase to all of the new tasks that go along with site-based budgeting. However, it is foreseeable that in an era of smooth, fully computerized budgeting, clerical support could be reduced to help free up funds for the core curricular areas.

Additional Sources of Funds
for Reallocation

The federal Comprehensive School Reform (CSR) grants also helped make school reform feasible for one of the schools in our study. This urban, Midwestern school received nearly $62,000 from the new grant program. It used these funds for professional development, specifically training teachers in ESL techniques, and increasing the number of bilingual aides, all of which were vital components of the school's reform model.

Some state grant programs also provided discretionary resources to schools undergoing reform efforts. We saw evidence that state reading grants helped enable schools to afford to implement the Success for All program. Although not representing a large amount of additional money, grant funds often provided the additional resources necessary for the schools to fully implement their educational strategies.

Another way in which the schools we studied were able to free up resources was to apply for waivers that allowed categorical funds to be used for other purposes. For example, one Midwestern school applied for a waiver in order to make it legal to serve certain classifications of special education students in the regular education classroom. Obtaining this waiver made the implementation of their inclusionary class-size reduction strategy possible. Similarly, another elementary school in the Midwest applied for a waiver in order to be deemed eligible to use their Title I funds for their schoolwide strategy of class-size reduction. This waiver was necessary because the school population was made up of only 35% low-income students, and the Title I law requires 50% or more in order to apply the funds to schoolwide programs. This is another example of how obtaining a waiver allowed the school to realize its educational vision.

Summary

In this chapter, we have categorized a typical school's staff into six categories and discussed where research suggests resources are being reallocated. We have talked about the specific changes that schools made, that is, what they "traded in" to afford the components of their new educational strategy. These examples show that by reallocating from all categories of staff as well as by obtaining grants and waivers, schools can free up a substantial amount of money for their new educational vision. In the next chapter, we choose a couple of sites to examine in more detail as a way of summarizing the resource reallocation that we have studied. We look at exactly what they reallocated in order to purchase all of the elements of their new strategy, and we examine how those changes have affected student achievement. We also take a step back and look at the district context in which these schools are located, revealing clues as to how districts can support these fundamentally important reform efforts.

CHAPTER SIX

Step 6:

Effects of Resource Reallocation and District Roles to Support Such Changes

Many studies have shown that the most successful reforms are results focused. As we have discussed in this book, the main reason that schools engage in reform and reallocate resources is to boost student achievement. Therefore, in order to assess the success of the changes undertaken by the schools studied, it is necessary to track the changes they have produced in student achievement. This chapter describes in some detail the performance improvements produced at two schools: one that implemented an inclusionary model with reduced class sizes, and one that implemented the Success for All reading program, requiring them to hire teacher tutors and an instructional facilitator, as well as invest in extensive professional development. For each, we discuss the details of how they reallocated dollars to fund their program reforms, and then we examine the effects that those reforms had on student achievement. After these more extensive school profiles, we provide additional evidence of student achievement gains from similar reforms implemented at other sites.

Finally, although the changes at the school level should be the thrust of any study of resource reallocation, one cannot ignore the reality that all schools function within a district context. The decisions that districts make with regard to how schools are funded, whether reform efforts are encouraged and supported, changes that may need to be made at the district level to help schools function better—all of these district actions help determine the scope of the educational strategy that schools choose and the degree of success they achieve. This chapter concludes by drawing up a list of effective practices for districts interested in supporting school-level reform.

Reallocating Resources to Support Class Size Reduction

For the purpose of this discussion, we will refer to the school in the following example as Farnham Elementary School. Farnham Elementary School is located in a medium-sized urban district in the midwestern United States. The school serves only grades K-2 because it is paired with another elementary school serving grades 3-5. The student population of approximately 400 students is about 38% minority. Approximately 23% of all students qualify for ESL services, and 35% qualify for free or reduced-price lunch.

The principal at Farnham was largely responsible for instigating change. First and foremost, she was concerned about the school's low achievement scores: Farnham was one of 29 elementary schools in a district of 45 schools, and its students consistently scored in the lowest quarter of all elementary schools in the district. Second, the principal was concerned with the school's practices of pulling students with special needs out of the classroom for extra help. This included Title I, ESL, and special education students, none of whom were having much academic success in their current program. The principal at Farnham chose to address this concern over student learning by virtually eliminating pull-out programs, such as English as a Second Language (ESL) small group instruction and Title I remediation, and using those staff slots to hire classroom teachers to reduce class size to approximately 16. Both the principal and the teachers believed that they would be better able to serve all students in these smaller, more inclusive settings. In this way, she also managed to improve the continuity of the instructional program and increase the number of minutes that all students spent on reading. The next few paragraphs describe how she found the resources to make these changes.

To achieve the desired reduction in class size, the number of regular classroom teachers had to be increased by six. The resources to pay for those positions were largely reallocated from categorical funds that had been paying for all of the pull-out programs. These included 5.1 positions in all: The 1.1 Title I teacher, the 3.0 ESL teachers, the 0.4 minority achievement teacher called "RISE," the 0.2 Gifted and Talented teacher, and the 0.4 Supplemental teacher allotment were all reallocated to pay for regular classroom teachers. The school gained an additional classroom teacher because of an unexpected increase in enrollment, for a total of seven additional classroom teacher positions.

The school organized teachers into a series of two-teacher teams, each with about 32 to 34 students. Some of the groups were multiage (usually spanning 2 years), and some were the same age. Moreover, nearly all teams had two adjoining classrooms, which usually had an open wall between them. Finally, during reading, each team organized reading groups from all students in the two-teacher team grouping.

We should note that because this school had a low-income student population of only 35%, the principal had to obtain a waiver to use Title I funds for schoolwide purposes rather than the pull-out program. Predicting that she would need additional money for intensive professional development needed to help ensure quality implementation of the school's new educational strategy, the principal also applied for and received a Comprehensive School Reform (CSR) grant in the amount of $62,000 (for the first of three years). This money helped support that staff development, much of it focused on developing ESL teaching skills for all teachers, and is described in the next paragraph.

In order to accommodate students with special needs in the regular classroom, most of whom were ESL students, teachers needed to learn instructional strategies that would help them simultaneously teach content as well as language development, the latter a need for about one third of the students in most classrooms. The principal addressed this need with an intensive professional development program, offering classes in ESL instruction at the school site. This concentrated use of resources for professional development, approximately $15,000, was paid for with the money from the CSR grant. This was six times the amount of money spent on school-site professional development in the previous year. In using professional development dollars to give teachers additional skills, one of the resource allocation strategies employed at Farnham was to shift some of the functions that had been provided by the teachers who formerly taught in pull-out programs onto regular education classroom teachers.

Although the principal's goal was to have all of the teachers be dual licensed in regular education and ESL, she recognized that this could not happen immediately. Therefore, she began by making sure that there was at least one dual-certified teacher on each teacher team for the 1998-1999 school year and encouraged all teachers who were not dual certified to enroll in the professional development program. Over time, the principal expects the combination of attrition and a policy of hiring only teachers with dual certification will result in the school's having only dual-licensed staff for all teaching positions.

In order to make these changes at Farnham, the principal had to win the support of the superintendent and school board in her community. Although she was able to persuade them, she had to agree to have her students' achievement closely monitored so that the district could be sure that Farnham's new educational strategy was working. One condition of the district's approval was the submission of a yearly report by the school on students' academic performance under this program. The district also required the principal to make a yearly presentation to the school board on the implementation and effect of the program on Farnham students. And finally, the award of the next two years of the CSR grant was contingent upon the submission of a yearly report monitoring student progress. With the support of these agencies contingent on the results at Farnham, the principal had to be very specific in her plans for the assessment of the inclusionary class-size reduction model.

The main assessment being used to monitor student progress is a district test, the Primary Language Arts Assessment (PLAA). This district test is aligned with the state's list of academic standards, which is an outline of what students should know and be able to do by the fourth, eighth, and 12th grades. Because these tests are administered to young children who are just beginning to read and write, the format of the test includes a reading portion, as well as a "Words I Know" section, where students write as many words as they can in a specific time period (3 to 5 minutes).

However, because so many of the students at Farnham did not take the PLAA in the 1997-1998 school year, there were no baseline scores with which to compare the 1998-1999 scores. Therefore, the principal devised a system whereby the 1999 scores would be compared to the benchmarks set up by Reading Recovery, a program designed to help children who are struggling with reading. Ambitious goals were set for 1999 according to those benchmarks, and those goals were that 95% of first- and second-grade students would read at grade level, as measured by a Text Reading Level (TRL) of 16+ for first graders and 20+ for second graders. Although the school did not meet these goals in the first year—60% of first graders scored a TRL of 16 or higher, and 88% of second graders scored a 20 or higher—the principal found these scores encouraging because many more students were hitting the benchmark than had in the previous year. Furthermore, many more students (mainly ESL students) who were previously excluded from the test took it this first year, a victory in itself according to the principal. But the most important measure of the success of the new strategy will not be available until the end of the 2001-2002 school year, after those who were in kindergarten at Farnham for the first year of the new model take the third-grade reading test. The principal hopes that at least 95% of these students will be reading at grade level by third grade, thus reflecting the success of the new model.

Reallocating Resources to Fund Tutors, a Facilitator, and Professional Development

Hollister Elementary School (not its actual name) is a K-5 school serving approximately 511 children in Cordell Place School District, the suburban district in the northwestern United States that we mentioned in Chapter 1. The student population is approximately 49% minority. About 6% of the students receive special education services, and about 3% receive instruction in ESL. Approximately two thirds of the students are eligible for free or reduced-price lunch.

For many years, Hollister's students were among the lowest achievers in the district. The staff at Hollister found it increasingly difficult to teach the growing low-income population of students that attended their school, and they were hungry for a new curriculum. At the same time, a new superintendent came to the district, a man who shared Hollister's (and other schools') dissatisfaction with the persistently low achievement scores. As discussed in Chapter 1, the superintendent of this district decided to incite change by making an offer to all schools with more than 50% low-income students. He told them that if they would undergo a year of self-study to determine a research-based method of improving student achievement, they would be given full control over their Title I funds to use for their chosen strategy. (The self-study is described in detail in Chapter 1.) In order to ensure that the amount of Title I money that these schools received was substantial, the superintendent declared that all Title I remedial reading teacher and instructional aide positions would not exist the following school year. Instead, the Title I money used to fund those positions would be part of the lump sum of Title I money given to the schools that underwent the self-study and could be deployed for their new educational strategy.

Low reading scores were judged the most pressing problem by the Hollister staff, so the research-based strategy they selected was a reading program called Success for All (SFA). Implementing SFA (one of the more expensive reading programs on the market) required substantial reallocation of the school's resources. The main elements of the program are a full-time instructional facilitator, at least one certified teacher to serve as a reading tutor (plus one more full-time tutor for every 25% of students in poverty), a full-time family liaison, extensive professional development, and design-based instructional materials. The instructional facilitator and tutors were new expenditures for the school, and the professional development program and instructional materials (then about $50,000 and now about $70,000 for a school of 500 students) required dramatic increases in the amount of money the school spent for those purposes. The following paragraph describes how Hollister found the money to fund the program.

With the superintendent's elimination of the Title I remedial reading teachers, Hollister had the funds for two additional positions, and it used these funds to pay for the full-time instructional facilitator and the certified teacher tutor. Even if the superintendent had not made the decision to eliminate all Title I specialists, this would have been the most logical area from which to shift resources because the implementation of SFA eliminated the need for these resource room teachers. Still, it was probably easier for the school to make such a change because the superintendent did not give it a choice of using those funds the way they had been used.

Because Hollister had such a high percentage of low-income students, SFA recommended that the school hire two additional teacher tutors, but it could not find the money to do so. Instead, it used 13.0 hours per day of instructional aide time for one-on-one tutoring. The aide time used to provide tutoring was funded by a combination of Title I and a state reading grant that the school was awarded in the year that it implemented the SFA program. Although these aides had previously been employed at the school, using them to provide tutoring rather than as classroom support and funding them with Title I and grant funds rather than the general allocation represented a shift in the way those resources were being used. Although it is true that research has shown that aides performing the role of tutor are not as effective as certified teachers (Shanahan, 1998), the school felt that making this resource shift was the best it could do to fully implement the program. To cover the functions of the family liaison position required by the model, the school was able to use a position already in place, a full-time guidance counselor. To do this, the role of the counselor was expanded to include the family outreach and social services coordination functions embodied in the SFA family liaison position.

The professional development required for this program is extensive and involves not only a programmatic cost but also paying travel costs and hiring substitutes for teachers when they have to attend seminars. In addition, the school had to purchase special instructional materials for the program. In total, the school spent $35,000 on SFA-related professional development and materials: $12,000 of Title I funds were used to pay for the SFA contract, $14,500 of the state reading grant funds helped cover the costs of professional development, and $8,500 from a combination of Title I and the state reading grant funds were used to pay for the required instructional materials.

Cordell Place School District and Hollister Elementary School each put a comprehensive testing program in place to monitor and help ensure improved student achievement in the wake of these reforms. In the 1996-1997 school year, the California Test of Basic Skills (CTBS) scores were at 33% for reading and 27% for math. The following year, in 1997-1998, they rose to 46% in reading and 51% in math. In 1998-1999, the CTBS was not administered. Instead, the third graders were given the ITBS in April, and their scores on that test were 49% for reading and 49% for math. On the state achievement test given in April 1997, the reading score was 33.3%, and the math score was 3.9%. The next year, in April 1998, the reading score increased to 43.3%, and the math score rose to 15.2%. In 1999, the reading score dropped a bit to 39.7%, and the math score fell slightly to 13.4%. Even with these slight dips, the results represent substantial improvement.

Although these scores have not yet reached the statewide averages of 48% in reading and 22% in math, they have increased significantly. The principal credits the SFA reading program and the Math Wings program with having made all the difference in the world. She describes parents as being excited about the program as well. She also emphasizes that without the commitment of the staff to these initiatives that resulted from the year-long needs assessment, the school would not have seen such improvement.

Achievement Gains at Other Sites Undergoing Reform and Resource Reallocation

Around the country, schools are implementing these and other new educational strategies in an effort to boost the achievement of all students. For many such schools, it is early in their implementation process, but it is clear that progress is being made. New American Schools recently published a paper titled "Working Toward Excellence: Examining the Effectiveness of New American Schools Designs" (New American Schools, 1999). This paper gives the results up to this point from many schools that are implementing New American Schools Designs, and all are showing gains. The creators of SFA have conducted similar research that shows consistent gains when the program is implemented properly (Slavin & Madden, 1999; Slavin et al., 1994).

In addition to the two schools that we studied and discussed in detail in the previous section, we have studied three other schools that have also experienced achievement gains after implementing similar reforms. One of these schools implemented a class size reduction model; the other two adopted the SFA design, hired an instructional facilitator and tutors, and dramatically increased the money they spent on professional development. All of the schools we studied were pleased that the reforms had helped them make progress toward the ambitious goals of standards-based education reform. However, as the achievement data cited above shows, although they are making progress, these schools have a long way to go before all of their students are learning to the level of state and district performance standards. There are probably a variety of other changes that need to be made in order to achieve these goals, and undoubtedly, such dramatic changes take time.

These performance findings reinforce the comments made in Chapter 1 about the change process. Step 3 in the large-scale school change process is implementation, monitoring, and improvement. The above data suggest that the schools studied have made significant improvements in their students' academic performance. Thus, they have accomplished the short-term goals of their restructuring and resource reallocation efforts. But they have more progress to make. Most schools first need to ensure that they have fully implemented their new educational strategies. For example, a number of schools studied had continued to use aides for individual tutoring, but even when trained, aides serving as tutors have less impact on student performance than teacher tutors. Thus, one short-term objective for these schools could be to replace aides serving as tutors with fully licensed teacher tutors; such a change should provide another boost in student reading achievement.

Next, most schools need to examine whether they have implemented sufficient changes in all core curricular areas. Recall that most elementary schools devoted the first 2 to 3 years to improving their reading program and were just beginning to alter their math program in the year studied. They need to fully implement the mathematics improvements, and then move on to science and social studies.

Finally, schools need to continue to keep pace with the professional literature to learn of any and all new developments. It could be that within 5 years, even more powerful strategies will have been developed, perhaps even tapping the full instructional potential of computer technologies. Schools will then need to determine how to include these new and better instructional improvement efforts.

Moreover, as mentioned in Chapter 1, one of the factors that influences the success of school-based educational reforms is the support provided by the district in which the school is located. In the next section, we describe the kinds of support that districts can provide schools to help them achieve the goal of teaching all students to the level of high standards.

District Support for School-Level Reform and Resource Reallocation

Schools do not function in a vacuum. All public schools, except for charter schools, operate in a district context. Odden and Busch (1998) indicate the changed roles and functions for districts as they implement a school-based form of educational improvement. In this section, we briefly summarize some of the key supports that districts provided in helping schools engage in the program change and resource reallocation practices profiled in this book.

There are many different kinds of support that districts can provide to schools that engage in resource reallocation and school-level reform. We begin by discussing the importance of giving schools control over at least a portion of their budget. In doing so, we touch on the range of budgetary control that districts can give schools as well as other ways they can encourage schools to use their budgets differently. We then discuss the fact that it may be helpful for districts to provide some extra financial support to schools undergoing extensive reforms, not in lieu of, but as a complement to, encouraging resource reallocation of existing dollars. Another important support that districts can offer is up-to-date technology. For a school that has been given control over its budget, online access to budget and expenditure information for its site can mean the difference between fully using the power of budgetary control and an administrative nightmare. Finally, we describe the importance of districts providing ideological support for school-level reform. Without district leadership in these monumental changes to the way schools do business, schools are bound to be less successful in their reforms.

Granting schools budgetary control. Nearly all school designs, as well as class-size reduction, require school resources to be spent differently (Odden & Busch, 1998; Odden & Picus, 2000). Therefore, to implement these designs and strategies, schools must have control over at least a portion of their school budget. Without the ability to control a substantial portion of resources at the school site, school leaders are unable to make the sort of discretionary spending decisions that are necessary to shift resources to the strategies embedded in their new educational strategy. Even worse, without being able to consider using resources differently, the type of new educational strategy that schools can consider is quite limited (Richardson, 1998), and the schools end up retaining what they have while adding only marginal elements. This strategy usually produces neither significant program change nor significant resource reallocation, and often does not boost performance much either.

Fortunately, many districts are beginning to realize that schools must have some control over their budget in order to engage in meaningful school restructuring. As Edward Kelly, the superintendent of Prince William County (Virginia) Public Schools in 1989, put it, "We want our students to get the best education possible, and we know that the principal is in the best position to guarantee that school funds are spent wisely to meet this goal" (Neal, 1989, p. 16). Studies have shown a direct correlation between the amount of (unencumbered) funds budgeted to the school site and the district's commitment to real management of program and budget (Neal, 1994). Neal translates that to mean that close to 75% of the school district's operational budget should be under control of individual schools if the district is serious about school-based restructuring and resource reallocation.

The range of budgetary control enjoyed by the schools we studied was quite large. Some of the schools had control over only their Title I funds and any grant money they were able to garner, whereas in the second year of implementation, schools in the Cordell Place School District had control over their entire staff budgets as well as other discretionary resources. As a rule, those schools that were given more budgetary control also had more control over which reforms they adopted. The following paragraphs discuss the range of budgetary control that districts can grant schools to encourage resource reallocation and reform.

Even if districts are not quite ready to move to a site-based budgeting system where the majority of the school funds are allocated to the site in a lump sum, any district that wants to encourage resource reallocation can do so by first giving schools control over their Title I funds. Many districts have already done so, but some still control Title I funds at the district level and allocate staff to schools that are paid for with Title I funds. These staff members are usually remedial reading specialists, serving low-income students by pulling them out of their regular classroom and providing assistance, usually remedial reading and mathematics, in a resource room setting. As we mentioned several times in this book, the effectiveness of these pull-out strategies has been called into question (e.g., see Odden, 1991), and changes were made throughout the 1990s to allow schools to apply Title I funds to schoolwide programs. This gives schools a broader range of strategies on which to spend these funds.

One stimulus for using Title I dollars differently was the 1995 change in the eligibility rule for applying Title I funds to schoolwide programs. By enabling all schools with at least 50% of their students in poverty to apply Title I funds to schoolwide programs, the number of schools in this category now encompasses a much broader income range. Thus, for many schools, Title I funds represent a fairly large sum of money, formerly targeted to programs for low-income students alone, which schools can now apply to virtually any program. Even if this is the only pot of money over which districts allow schools control, for schools that meet the eligibility criteria for applying Title I funds to schoolwide programs, this can represent a substantial source of funding for resource reallocation and reform.

In Cordell Place, the superintendent began by giving some schools control over their Title I dollars. In the following year, the district moved those same schools to a complete site-based management system with a new school-based formula funding system (see http://www.wcer.wisc.edu/cpre/ pdfs.htm for a full case study on a school in this district). Because these schools were implementing research-based strategies as they had been encouraged to do by the superintendent, he believed that the logical next step was to give them the budgetary control they needed to fully implement and finance their new strategies.

Thus, a second fiscal support strategy would be for districts to provide schools with lump-sum budgets through needs-based funding formulas rather than, as is typically the case, providing sites with various types and levels of staffing resources through staffing formulas. Many districts around the country are implementing this school-based funding strategy as part of district efforts to encourage school-based restructuring and resource reallocation (Odden, 1999). School-based financing, which is a set of policies that includes both formula funding of schools as well as resource reallocation, is rapidly expanding across the country (Odden & Goertz, 1999) and the world (Levacic, Caldwell, Ross, & Odden, in press; Ross & Levacic, 1999).

In addition to providing schools a lump-sum budget and encouraging them to reallocate resources so that school funds support the most effective research-based educational strategies, districts can choose to make new rules governing the use of certain resources. This allows districts to maintain some control over how schools spend money, even if the district has given the school control over the majority of its budget. This strategy also helps schools make some of the harder personnel decisions. For example, in the Cordell Place School District, the superintendent decided that as part of the district's reform efforts, the position of Title I pull-out specialists would no longer exist. In doing so, the superintendent forced the schools that had recently gained control over their Title I budgets to rethink how that money would be spent. Having pushed the use of research-based school designs, he encouraged schools to put the money that previously funded these pull-out, remedial reading specialists toward the funding of instructional facilitators, reading tutors, and other proven-effective positions. It is this sort of push from district leadership that sometimes may be necessary to embolden schools to make those difficult changes that may make the critical difference in improving academic achievement.

Providing schools with financial support for reform. Although the focus of this book is on resource reallocation of existing school resources, it may be a good idea for districts to set up an investment fund to help schools pay for some of the up-front costs of comprehensive school reform. There are many reasons why a district might want to offer such financial support. For one, low-achieving schools in need of comprehensive school reform may require such a district investment in order to improve. Many changes can be made at such schools by performing a needs assessment, choosing research-based remedies, and allowing school leaders to reallocate resources to the areas of greatest need, but the school might need some additional stimulus to engage in this complex effort. A district first-year investment pool could constitute this type of stimulus.

As an example of low-achieving schools that required additional up-front resources, we studied two schools in one midwestern district that were being reconstituted because of persistently low achievement scores. This district funded the students at those schools at a higher weight than the other students in that district. In this way, the district illustrated its belief that in order to raise student achievement, these schools needed more than just the ability to reallocate existing resources. This district was planning to increase the funding for all schools in the future, but it was willing to provide the increased funding first to the schools most in need of improvement.

Using technology to support school-level reform. Another way that a district can help support a school's resource reallocation and educational reform process is by providing up-to-date technology that allows schools to calculate their actual budgets in the simplest manner possible and monitor expenditures on a real-time basis. Ideally, schools would be able to log on to a centrally maintained site that contained their budgets when any sort of change needed to be made. This would be even more efficient than allowing schools to maintain their own budgets because it allows the district to include actuals for salaries, operations, maintenance, utilities, and transportation. Such a process is being implemented in the Cordell Place School District. In the meantime, although schools in Cordell Place cannot access their budgets online, they are all connected to a central network, which gives them access to much of the same information.

The business manager in Cordell Place has also set up a computer program, called Budget Assistant, that schools can open up at their site and use to help create their budget for the next school year. This program uses prompts to move the user through a database-driven system, linking the decisions that the user at the school site makes with actual financial figures for those decisions, thereby helping the user create an accurate budget for that school. Also, because schools need an up-to-date version of their current expenditures throughout the school year, the business manager sends each school an updated report on the 15th of every month. Eventually, this information will be available online and will then be completely current every day of the month; but until that time, schools expressed appreciation that at least once a month, they knew exactly where they stood financially. Principals in this district repeatedly told us what a difference these technological supports make in their effort to reallocate resources in order to boost student achievement.

More examples of these computer systems exist around the country and beyond. Seattle has this type of computer system up and running (http://sps.gspa.washington.edu/sps/budget.html), and several other districts and states in the country are developing such systems. Internationally, Victoria, Australia has also created this type of automated fiscal system (Odden, 1999), which includes automated invoicing and purchase ordering.

Ideological support for school-level reform. As important as the monetary support is the ideological support for school reform. In a study of schools implementing New American Schools (NAS) designs, Susan Bodilly found that district support, or lack thereof, could either promote or derail a school's reform efforts. "Schools looked to district leadership and climate to understand if it was worth their while to invest time and effort in transforming," Bodilly said (Richardson, 1998, p. 55).

This was true in our research as well. When the new superintendent brought reform to Cordell Place, he made it clear that the motto of this new central office would be "We're here to serve." And this was not just a rhetorical statement. All of the district administrators were committed to the reform process, even to the extent that they were willing to put in long hours at the school site helping schools with their chosen new educational strategies. The superintendent did not just require a yearlong needs-assessment process, which was a sign in itself of the district's commitment to reform, but he also provided the schools with help in analyzing their data and researching strategies that could help turn student achievement around at their schools. After schools had completed most of their needs assessment and begun researching school designs, he encouraged school leaders to attend an organized design fair, where they learned more about which strategies might be appropriate for their particular needs. All of these supports, in combination with giving schools substantial budgetary control, forcing certain changes, and providing incentives to make others, are good examples of how a district can give its schools the technical and psychological support they need to engage in the difficult tasks of program restructuring and resource reallocation.

In the district where we studied the two schools that were reconstituted, ideological support for reform was equally important. When a school is reconstituted, there is a sense of failure on the part of the old school staff as well as district administrators and community members. Positive district leadership can make the difference between hiring a new, energized staff that is committed to turning the school around and merely hiring a new staff that feels destined to fail as the old one did. The process in place in the district we studied ensured that the strategies chosen for the reconstituted school were appropriate for the needs of those students. Furthermore, the district carefully selected a principal and lead teachers who believed in these new strategies and who were committed to selecting an entire staff devoted to improvement. Finally, this district helped galvanize the community to support the school's reform efforts by involving them in the reform process and making them believe that this school that had failed their children would become a high-achieving school. This sort of district leadership is critical to the success of any long-term school restructuring process.

Conclusion

Assessing the results of the strategies that schools put in place in an effort to raise student achievement is fundamentally important. After all, what good is resource reallocation to support new school strategies if those strategies do not lead to the desired improvements in student achievement? When reforms are successful, districts can help schools remain committed to their efforts by celebrating their successes and showing their continued support for the changes that those schools are making. Similarly, when reforms are not as successful as school and district leaders had hoped, districts can help schools analyze what may not be working and help redirect their efforts. As we explained in Chapter 1, monitoring reform efforts and continually looking for ways to improve is an important part of the change process that schools must go through to achieve their goals.

In this book, we have shown that resource reallocation is not just using school funds differently. Rather, it is part of a long-term, large-scale process in which the school essentially changes all of its major features—beginning with its overall instructional program and a new strategy for struggling students, and moving on to include class size, student grouping, organization of teacher time, professional development, and, along with these changes, its use of all of its staffing and other fiscal resources.

This book has profiled the restructuring efforts of several schools and has shown that there are common themes running through the resource reallocation practices in which schools engaged during the 1990s. We believe that these resource reallocation practices are significant, were difficult to produce in each school, and should continue to result in improvements in student performance.

We also know that this type of program restructuring and resource reallocation is possible in many more schools in the United States. Odden (1997a) showed how this was possible for most of the schools in districts that had partnered with the New American Schools. Odden and Picus (2000) show how these restructuring possibilities vary by region of the country because average funding levels differ across the country. And Odden and Archibald (in press) show that this type of significant resource reallocation is possible even for some of the lowest spending districts in one midwestern state. Finally, Odden (in press) details the costs of a full-fledged comprehensive school design, which again is affordable by many schools if they are willing to engage in program restructuring and resource reallocation.

We also believe that there might be even more resource reallocation efforts in the first decade of this next century. As might be evident from the lack of mention, few of the schools studied made extensive instructional uses of computer technologies. As this option becomes more possible in the future, we expect even more dramatic resource reallocation to accommodate all of these changes. Until that time, we hope that more and more schools engage in the fundamental restructuring that the schools in this book have attempted. At the very least, this process leads them to examine their current use of resources and reallocate them to the most effective strategies for boosting student performance. And by doing so, they have begun the professional practice of matching resource use with the deployment of best practices. Thus, as newer and even better practices emerge in the future, some of which just might include more integrated uses of computer technologies, these schools may be best prepared to engage in another round of resource reallocation to put these new practices in place. This sort of continuous evolution and improvement, after all, is the mark of a professional and performance-oriented school.

Resources on the Internet

Following is a listing of the World Wide Web resources found throughout the book:

Center for Social Organization of Schools (http://www.csos.jhu.edu/default1.htm)

Talent Development High Schools (http://www.csos.jhu.edu/Talent/high.htm)

Talent Development Middle Schools (http://www.csos.jhu.edu/Talent/middle.htm)

Consortium for Policy Research in Education (http://www.wcer.wisc.edu/cpre/)

Edison Schools (http://www.edisonschools.com)

Expeditionary Learning/Outward Bound (http://www.elob.org/)

Modern Red Schoolhouse (http://www.mrsh.org/)

National Center on Education and the Economy (http://www.ncee.org/)

America's Choice (http://www.ncee.org/ac/intro.html)

New American Schools (http://naschools.org)

Northwest Regional Educational Laboratory (http://www.nwrel.org/)

Chicago Mathematics (http://www.nwrel.org/scpd/natspec/catalog/univchicago.htm)

First Steps (http://www.nwrel.org/scpd/natspec/catalog/firstsetps.htm)

Catalog of School Designs (http://www.nwrel.org/scpd/natspec/catalog/index.html)

Seattle Public Schools (http://sps.gspa.washington.edu/sps/budget.html)

Southern Regional Education Board (http://www.sreb.org/)

High Schools That Work (http://www.sreb.org/Programs/hstw/high.html)

Success for All (http://www.successforall.net/)

TERCworks (http://www.tercworks.terc.edu/)

REFERENCES

Achilles, C. (1999). *Let's put kids first, finally: Getting class size right.* Thousand Oaks, CA: Corwin.

Analt, B., Goertz, M., & Turnbull, B. (1999). *Implementing whole school reform in New Jersey: Year One in the first cohort schools.* New Brunswick: Rutgers, The State University of New Jersey, Edward J. Bloustein School of Planning and Public Policy.

Beck, L., & Murphy, J. (1996). *The four imperatives of a successful school.* Thousand Oaks, CA: Corwin.

Borman, G. D., & D'Agostino, J. V. (1996). Title I and student achievement: A meta-analysis of federal evaluation results. *Educational Evaluation and Policy Analysis, 18,* 309-326.

Bradley, A., Hoff, D. J., & Manzo, K. K. (1999). Teachers support most standards-based changes. *Education Week, 19(9),* 8.

Campbell, J., Voelkl, K., & Donahue, P. (1998). *NAEP 1996 trends in academic progress.* Washington, DC: U.S. Department of Education.

Cohen, D. K., & Hill, H. (1998). *State policy and classroom performance: Mathematics reform in California* (Policy Brief RB-23). Philadelphia: University of Pennsylvania, Consortium for Policy Research in Education.

Comer, J. P., Haynes, N. M., Joyner, E. T., & Ben-Avie, M. (1996). *Rallying the whole village: The Comer process for reforming education.* New York: Teachers College Press.

Cooper, R., Slavin, R. E., & Madden, N. A. (1997, April). *Success for all: Exploring the technical, normative, political and socio-cultural dimensions of scaling up.* Paper presented at the annual meetings of the American Educational Research Association, Chicago.

Darling-Hammond, L. (1996). Restructuring schools for high performance. In S. Fuhrman & J. O'Day (Eds.), *Rewards and reform: Creating educational incentives that work* (pp. 144-192). San Francisco: Jossey-Bass.

Elmore, R., & Burney, D. (1996). *Professional development and instructional improvement in Community School District #2, New York City.* Philadelphia: University of Pennsylvania, Consortium for Policy Research in Education.

Elmore, R., & Peterson, P. (1996). *Restructuring in the classroom: Teaching, learning and school organization.* San Francisco: Jossey-Bass.

Farkas, G. (1998). Reading one-to-one: An intensive program serving a great many students while still achieving. In J. Crane (Ed.), *Social programs that work.* New York: Russell Sage.

Farkas, G. (1999). *Can Title I attain its goal?* Brookings Papers on Education Policy. Washington, DC: The Brookings Institution.

Finn, J., & Achilles, C. (1999). Tennessee's class size study: Findings, implications, misconceptions. *Educational Evaluation and Policy Analysis, 21*(2), 97-109.

Finnan, C., St. John, E., McCarthy, J., & Slovacek, S. (1996). *Accelerated schools in action.* Thousand Oaks, CA: Corwin.

Fowler, W., & Walberg, H. (1991). School size, characteristics and outcomes. *Educational Evaluation and Policy Analysis, 13,* 189-202.

Fuchs, D., & Fuchs, L. (1994-1995). Sometimes separate is better. *Educational Leadership, 52*(4), 22-26.

Gamoran, A., Porter, A. C., Smithson, J., & White, P. A. (1997). Upgrading high school mathematics instruction: Improving learning opportunities for low-income, low-achieving youth. *Educational Evaluation and Policy Analysis, 19,* 325-338.

Grissmer, D. (Ed.). (1999). Class size: Issues and new findings [Special issue]. *Educational Evaluation and Policy Analysis, 21*(2).

Haynes, N., Emmons, C., & Woodruff, D. (1998). School development program effects: Linking implementation to outcomes. *Journal of Education for Students Placed At Risk, 3*(1), 71-85.

Herman, R. (1999). *An educator's guide to schoolwide reform.* Arlington, VA: Educational Research Service.

Hirsch, E. D. (1996). *The schools we need and why we don't have them.* New York: Doubleday.

Howley, C. (1989). Synthesis of the effects of school and district size: What research says about achievement in small schools and school districts. *Journal of Rural and Small Schools, 4*(1), 2-12.

Huberman, M., & Miles, M. (1984). *Innovation up close.* New York: Plenum.

Joyce, B., & Showers, B. (1998). *Student achievement through staff development.* New York: Longman.

King, M. B., & Newmann, F. M. (1999). *School capacity as a goal for professional development: Mapping the terrain in low-income schools.* Paper prepared for the Consortium for Policy Research in Education, University of Wisconsin–Madison.

Lankford, H., & Wyckoff, J. (1995). Where has the money gone? An analysis of school district spending in New York. *Educational Evaluation and Policy Analysis, 17,* 195-218.

Lee, V., Bryk, A., & Smith, J. (1993). The organization of effective secondary schools. In L. Darling-Hammond (Ed.), *Review of research in education* (Vol. 19, pp. 171-268). Washington, DC: American Educational Research Association.

Lee, V., & Smith, J. (1997). High school size: Which works best, and for whom? *Educational Evaluation and Policy Analysis, 19,* 205-228.

Levacic, R., Caldwell, B., Ross, K., & Odden, A. (in press). Funding schools by formula: Comparing practice in five countries. *Journal of Education Finance.*

Loucks-Horsley, S., Hewson, P., Love, N., & Stiles, K. (1998). *Designing professional development for teachers of science and mathematics.* Thousand Oaks, CA: Corwin.

Miles, K. H., & Darling-Hammond, L. (1998). Rethinking the allocation of teaching resources: Some lessons from high-performing schools. *Educational Evaluation and Policy Analysis, 20,* 9-29.

Mohrman, S. A. (1994). Making the transition to high-performance management. In S. A. Mohrman, P. Wohlstetter, & Associates (Eds.), *School-based management* (pp. 187-214). San Francisco: Jossey-Bass.

Mohrman, S. A., & Cummings, T. G. (1989). *Self-designing organizations: Learning how to create high performance.* Reading, MA: Addison-Wesley.

Molnar, A., Smith, P., Zahorik, J., Palmer, A., Halbach, A., & Ehrle, K. (1999). Evaluating the SAGE program: A pilot program in targeted pupil-teacher reduction in Wisconsin. *Educational Evaluation and Policy Analysis, 21,* 165-177.

Murnane, R., & Levy, F. (1996). *Teaching the new basic skills.* New York: Free Press.

Murphy, J., & Beck, L. (1995). *School-based management as school reform.* Thousand Oaks, CA: Corwin.

National Commission on Excellence and Equity in Education. (1983). *A nation at-risk: The imperative of educational reform.* Washington, DC: U.S. Department of Education.

Neal, R. (1989). School-based management lets principals slice the budget pie. *The Executive Educator, 11*(1), 16-19.

Neal, R. (1994). School-based management: The advantages of lump sum transfers. *School Business Affairs, 60*(6), 34-38.

New American Schools. (1999). *Working toward excellence: Examining the effectiveness of New American Schools designs.* Available: http://www.naschools.org/resource/publications.html.

Newmann, F. (1996). *Authentic achievement: Restructuring schools for intellectual quality.* San Francisco: Jossey-Bass.

Newmann, F., Lopez, G., & Bryk, A. (1998). *The quality of intellectual work in Chicago schools: A baseline report.* Chicago: Consortium on Chicago School Research.

Odden, A. (Ed.). (1991). *Education policy implementation.* Albany: State University of New York Press.

Odden, A. (1997a). *The finance side of implementing New American Schools.* Paper prepared for the New American Schools, Alexandria, VA.

Odden, A. (1997b). Having to do more with less: Stretching the school budget dollar. *School Business Affairs, 63*(6), 2-10.

Odden, A. (1997c). *A policymaker's guide to incentives for students, teachers and schools.* Denver, CO: Education Commission of the States.

Odden, A. (1999). Case Study 3: School based formula funding in North America. In K. Ross & R. Levacic (Eds.), *Needs-based resource allocation in schools via formula-based funding.* Paris: UNESCO, International Institute for Educational Planning.

Odden, A. (in press). Costs of sustaining educational change via comprehensive school reform. *Phi Delta Kappan.*

Odden, A., & Archibald, S. (in press). Reallocating resources to support higher student achievement: An empirical look at five sites. *Journal of Education Finance.*

Odden, A., Archibald, S., & Tychsen, A. (1999). *Can Wisconsin schools afford comprehensive school reform?* Madison: University of Wisconsin, Wisconsin Center for Education Research, Consortium for Policy Research in Education.

Odden, A., & Busch, C. (1998). *Financing schools for high performance: Strategies for improving the use of educational resources.* San Francisco: Jossey-Bass.

Odden, A., & Goertz, M. (Eds.). (1999). *School-based financing.* Thousand Oaks, CA: Corwin.

Odden, A., Monk, D., Nakib, Y., & Picus, L. (1995). The story of the education dollar: No Academy Awards and no fiscal smoking guns. *Phi Delta Kappan, 77,* 161-168.

Odden, A., & Picus, L. O. (2000). *School finance: A policy perspective* (2nd ed.). New York: McGraw-Hill.

Office of Educational Research and Improvement. (1996). *The uses of time for teaching and learning* (Studies of Education Reform). Washington, DC: U.S. Department of Education.

O'Neil, J. (1995). Finding time to learn. *Educational Leadership, 53*(4), 11-15.

Pisapia, J., & Westfall, L. (1996). *Alternative high school scheduling: Student achievement and behavior: Executive summary.* Richmond: Virginia Commonwealth University, Metropolitan Educational Research Consortium.

Raywid, M. A. (1997/1998). Synthesis of research: Small schools: A reform that works. *Educational Leadership, 55*(4), 34-39.

Rettig, M., & Canady, R. (1999). The effects of block scheduling. *School Administrator, 56*(3), 14-20.

Reynolds, A. J., & Wolfe, B. (1999). Special education and school achievement: An exploratory analysis with a central-city sample. *Educational Evaluation and Policy Analysis, 21,* 249-269.

Richardson, J. (1998). Reform by design can succeed. *Journal of Staff Development, 19*(3), 54-55.

Ross, K., & Levacic, R. (Eds.). (1999). *Needs-based resource allocation in schools via formula-based funding.* Paris: UNESCO, International Institute for Educational Planning.

Ross, S. M., Sanders, W., & Stringfield, S. (1998). *The Memphis restructuring initiative: Achievement results for Years 1 and 2 on the Tennessee value-added assessment system: A special report prepared for the Memphis City Schools.* Memphis, TN: Memphis City Schools.

Rothstein, R., & Miles, K. H. (1995). *Where has the money gone? Changes in the level and composition of education spending.* Washington, DC: Economic Policy Institute.

Sack, J. L. (1999). Debate turns on role of Title I aides: One Colorado district takes drastic action. *Education Week, 19*(14), 1, 26-27.

Schmidt, W. H., McKnight, C. C., & Raizen, S. A. (1997). *A splintered vision: An investigation of U.S. science and mathematics education.* Dordrecht, The Netherlands: Kluwer.

Shanahan, T. (1998). On the effectiveness and limitations of tutoring in reading. In L. Darling-Hammond (Ed.), *Review of research in education* (Vol. 23, pp. 217-234). Washington, DC: American Educational Research Association.

Sizer, T. (1996). *Horace's hope.* Boston: Houghton Mifflin.

Slavin, R. (1987). Ability grouping and student achievement in elementary schools: A best evidence synthesis. *Review of Educational Research, 57,* 293-336.

Slavin, R. (1990). Achievement effects of ability grouping in secondary schools: A best evidence synthesis. *Review of Educational Research, 60,* 471-499.

Slavin, R. (1993). Ability grouping in the middle grades: Achievement effects and alternatives. *Elementary School Journal, 93,* 535-552.

Slavin, R., & Fashola, O. (1998). *Show me the evidence! Proven and promising programs for America's schools.* Thousand Oaks, CA: Corwin.

Slavin, R., & Karweit, N. (1985). Effects of whole class, ability grouped and individualized instruction on mathematics achievement. *American Educational Research Journal, 22,* 351-357.

Slavin, R., Karweit, N., & Madden, N. (1989). *Effective programs for students at risk.* Newton, MA: Allyn & Bacon.

Slavin, R., & Madden, N. A. (1999). *Success for All/Roots and Wings: 1999 summary of research on achievement outcomes.* Available: http://www.successforall.net/sumresch99.html.

Slavin, R. E., Madden, N. A., Dolan, L., Wasik, B. A., Ross, S. M., & Smith, L. J. (1994). "Whenever and wherever we choose": The replication of Success for All. *Phi Delta Kappan, 75,* 639-647.

Stringfield, S., & Datnow, A. (Eds.). (1998). Scaling up school restructuring and improvement designs [Special issue]. *Education and Urban Society, 30*(3).

Stringfield, S., Ross, S., & Smith, L. (1996). *Bold plans for school restructuring: The New American Schools designs.* Mahway, NJ: Lawrence Erlbaum.

Traub, J. (1999). *Better by design? A consumer's guide to schoolwide reform.* Washington, DC: Thomas B. Fordham Foundation.

Tyack, D., & Cuban, L. (1996). *Tinkering toward utopia.* Cambridge, MA: Harvard University Press.

U.S. Department of Education's Mathematics and Science Expert Panel. (1999). *Exemplary & promising mathematics programs.* Washington, DC: U.S. Department of Education.

Veenman, S. (1995). Cognitive and noncognitive effects of multigrade and multi-age classes: A best evidence synthesis. *Review of Educational Research, 65,* 319-381.

Viadero, D. (1999). Education department is set to release its list of recommended math programs. *Education Week, 19*(6), 1, 14-15.

Vinovskis, M. (1999). Do federal compensatory education programs really work? A brief historical analysis of Title I and Head Start. *American Journal of Education, 107,* 187-209.

Wasik, B. A., & Slavin, R. (1993). Preventing early reading failure with one-to-one tutoring: A review of five programs. *Reading Research Quarterly, 28,* 178-200.

INDEX

Office of Educational Research and
Improvement, 41
O'Neil, J., 36
Online resources, 91-92
Organizational change, large-scale, 11,
19-20
creating new educational strategy,
11, 14-17
implementation/monitoring/
continuous improvement, 11,
17-29
needs assessment, 11-14
stages in, 11-20
time required, 19
Organizational/staffing issues,
31-32, 45
creating planning/professional development time, 31-32, 36-43
determining regular class size,
32-36
school size, 43-45

Palmer, A., 51
Peterson, P., 22
Picus, L., 60, 61
Picus, L. O., 32, 47, 48, 83, 89
Pisapia, J., 36
Porter, A. C., 54
Primary Language Arts Assessment
(PLAA), 77
Principals, 14
resource reallocation role, 1
Productivity improvement impera-
tive, 2-3
"Professional communities," 29-30
Professional development. *See* Teacher
professional development
Proficiency, NAEP definition of, 2
Pull-out resource room strategy, 4
eliminating, 16
eliminating ESL, 29
reducing, 16
Pull-out programs:
eliminating, 64, 75, 85

questioning effectiveness of, 62,
75, 84
Title I-supported, 62
Pull-out teachers:
dual-licensed, 16, 77
moving to regular classrooms,
16, 77
Pupil support specialists, 63
elimination of, 69
guidance counselors, 63, 69
nurses, 63
psychologists, 63
resource reallocation and, 69-70

Raizen, S. A., 22
Raywid, M. A., 43
Reading programs, 14, 23, 65, 69, 78,
79, 81
phonics-based, 16
See also specific reading programs
Reading Recovery program, 69, 78
Regular education specialists, 62
funding for, 65-66
See also Teachers
Resource reallocation, 1-3, 19-20, 73
case studies, 6, 10-11
district-level, 59-61
reasons to engage in, 3-5, 10
school-level, 61-63
sources of funds for, 72-73
Resource room services, retaining
some, 55
Rettig, M., 36
Reynolds, A. J., 48
Richardson, J., 83, 87
Roots and Wings program, 7, 18, 23,
49, 67
WWW address, 92
See also Talent Development
High Schools program; Talent
Development Middle Schools
program
Ross, K., 85
Ross, S., 5, 23, 25, 30, 44, 47

CORWIN
PRESS

The Corwin Press logo—a raven striding across an open book—represents the happy union of courage and learning. We are a professional-level publisher of books and journals for K–12 educators, and we are committed to creating and providing resources that embody these qualities. Corwin's motto is "Success for All Learners."